"Her tone is accessible to general readers . . . The stories of White's interviewees paint a textured, harrowing picture of high school life."   —*Publishers Weekly*

"A fascinating and troubling snapshot of a particualarly noxious and omnipresent experience of white, suburban girlhood."
—*San Francisco Chronicle*

"White isn't afraid to bust a few caps in the direction of sisterhood and apple pie . . . well-paced and well-written . . . *Fast Girls* makes a powerful case that as long as teenage girls are saddled with sexual canards, adult women will struggle with sexual injustices."   —*The San Diego Union-Tribune*

"Examines the phenomenon of the high school slut as an example of modern mythmaking . . . White's interviews are compellingly retold."   —*The Ledger* (Lakeland, FL)

"Because she takes her work seriously, White writes convincingly of the long-range effects of being branded a slut. She ends on a hope that bringing the slut story into consciousness will release its archetypal grip."   —*St Louis Post-Dispatch*

continued . . .

"White is the first to combine different methodologies in an attempt to write specifically about the function and significance of the teenage slut—in her words, 'to shed some light on that space in the high school hallway where so many vital and troubling encounters occur.'"
—*The Nation*

"Calling a young woman a slut may be a way of shutting her down, but Emily White opens up the term until it turns into a magical hall of mirrors, revealing all the ways in which fear of female power still shapes our culture. Ranking with the groundbreaking work of the *Second Wave*, much fiercer than most of what passes for feminist writing now, *Fast Girls* takes the discussion of the politics of sex to the next level." —Ann Powers, author of *Weird Like Us*

"A book for girls, boys, men and women." —*Los Angeles Times*

"Emily White's marvelous investigation of the 'myth of the slut' brings high school back in vivid color and shows how its tribal outcasts get scarred for life by the cruelty of the mob."
—Gary Indiana, author of *Let It Bleed* and *Resentment*

"In the end, *Fast Girls* does something breathtakingly simple. It presents the slut story from the point of view of the so-called slut." —*The Atlanta Journal-Constitution*

FAST GIRLS

TEENAGE TRIBES AND
THE MYTH OF THE SLUT

EMILY WHITE

BERKLEY BOOKS, NEW YORK

B

A Berkley Book
Published by The Berkley Publishing Group
A division of Penguin Group (USA) Inc.
375 Hudson Street
New York, New York 10014

The stories told in this work are based on personal experience and on interviews and correspondence with those portrayed. In most instances, however, the names and identifying details of individuals and places, whether noted in the text or not, have been changed.

PRINTING HISTORY
Scribner hardcover edition / March 2002
Berkley trade paperback edition / October 2003

Library of Congress Cataloging-in-Publication Data

White, Emily, 1966–
    Fast girls : teenage tribes and the myth of the slut / Emily White.
        p. cm.
    Originally published: New York : Scribner, 2002.
    ISBN 0-425-19176-1
    1. Teenagers—United States—Social life and customs. 2. High school students—United States—Social life and customs. 3. Teenage girls—Sexual behavior—United States—Public opinion. 4. Promiscuity—United States— Public opinion. 5. Gossip—United States. 6. Social isolation—United States. 7. High school environment—United States. I. Title: Myth of the slut. II. Title.

HQ796.W4726 2003
305.235'0973—dc21

                                                                    2003044443

PRINTED IN THE UNITED STATES OF AMERICA

10 9 8 7 6 5 4 3 2 1

To Josephine

Contents

Introduction

Maybe this story begins in Portland, Oregon, in the fall of 1980, when Anna Thomas enters Washington High as a freshman. She's one unit in a shipment of 250 freshman girls. She's one name on a list.

Washington is a public school with a population of about two thousand students, mostly upper-middle-class white kids, except for those bused in from minority neighborhoods, or the random few who, through some accident of zoning, have ended up among kids of a different economic tribe. Anna's presence at Washington is part of this accident of zoning. Though she lives with her mom in an apartment in the same zip code as the rich kids, she is by no means a rich kid. She can't afford the clothes most girls at Washington wear. She wears the knockoff versions of designer jeans and she eats government-assisted lunches. In the midst of a predominantly white student body she's half Filipina. She's exotic:

her skin vibrates with the color of another world. Add to this the fact that her breasts have developed much quicker than most girls', that her mom is a waitress, that she doesn't have many girlfriends, and Anna's presence is a recipe for scandal.

Kids start spreading rumors about Anna on the first day of school, and by winter she's infamous. She is now called Anna Wanna. *Anna wants* every guy she can touch, Anna will do anything, Anna is the biggest slut ever born.

The rumors surrounding Anna are as elaborate and meticulous as fairy tales. Reliable sources claim she has lain down with boys or men in an infinite number of places: graveyards, the empty lot where kids throw keggers on weekends, some guy's basement, some guy's car. Ask her to go into a closet or a bathroom and pull her shirt off and she'll do it—she'll pull herself apart at the slightest provocation. She'll lie on her back saying, "I love you," no matter who the guy is or where he has come from.

According to what everyone says and writes on the walls, Anna is a monster of desire, a freak of nature, an aberration. No one knows her very well, but the idea of her takes up a lot of space. When she walks down the hall, a murmur takes shape, irrepressible in the throats of all the kids. Sometimes one distinct voice emerges, shouting over the tide of whispers: *"Whore! Anna Wanna is a whore!"*

For the most part Anna keeps her cool. She continues her progress through the hall, staring straight ahead. Occasionally she swirls around, yells, *"Fuck you,"* and then there's the inevitable comeback: *"I already fucked you!"* After a confrontation like this her face reddens, and she looks as if she's on the verge—as if at any moment she might dissolve, her feet might curl up, like the witch killed by the flying house in *The Wizard of Oz.*

From where I sit her hair seems darker than midnight. I am part of the same army of freshman girls Anna belongs to, but unlike Anna I'm not the kind of girl who attracts attention. Even when you look right at me, it's easy to look past me. I'm a well-behaved, unobtrusive goody-goody: on the honor roll but not too high up, involved in a Save the Whales club, one or two friends, pushing every symptom of rage or desire or wild ambition down past the throat, down past the heart, all the way down into my guts.

I watch Anna swirl around and battle the catcalls and the predators; I find it difficult to take my eyes off her. Maybe because of my particular kind of invisibility, I become fascinated by Anna's infamy—the stories of sex and abandon and inappropriate kisses. When she's absent, which is often, school is far more boring than usual.

Long after high school has ended, I still dream about her. Like a kid obsessed in the hallway, I can't let go of the question of Anna and her true nature. Through the lens of memory, she becomes representative of a more generalized sense of chaos—moments when the good, orderly world you thought you knew falls away and a cruel reality begins to manifest itself. Anna and the rumors surrounding her seem to hold a clue to the past: Why did we want to talk this way? Why did we so effortlessly and automatically create a "slut," almost as if she were creating us? And why did we need to banish certain girls, push them out beyond the pale?

Sometimes, in those conversations about high school that people in their twenties and thirties engage in more and more frequently, I'd bring up the question of the slut. Invariably, my Anna stories would be countered by stories of other versions of her: other girls whose alleged insatiable sexual appetites scandalized their school, girls whose bodies had no boundaries.

One friend remembers Donuthole, the girl everyone said had been completely worn out from so much sex. A guy remembers Blow Job Brenda and the way she was supposed to have invited the wrestling team home with her to be serviced. At Thanksgiving, every member of my family has some story about the "loose" girl, with the exception of my sister's quiet boyfriend, who can't bring himself to tell the story. He simply says, "Oh yes, Sharon Suttelmeier," and nods gravely, mysteriously.

Gathering more and more anecdotes, I began to see similarities in the stories of the high school slut. Generally she was remembered by her first and last name and by her nicknames; she was remembered immediately, and often with regret; the stories surrounding her often focused on images of oral sex with multiple partners; and very few who participated in ostracizing her knew what had become of her. Often her fate after high school took on the sheen of stereotype. "I heard she was living in a basement with a coke dealer," one friend told me. Funny, I'd heard almost the exact same story about Anna Wanna.

It became clear to me that the story I had attributed to Anna was actually rooted somewhere in the collective unconscious. Like an urban legend, the slut story proved remarkably similar across time and geography—a sixty-four-year-old woman and a thirteen-year-old boy I spoke with told virtually

the same story of a girl who would give blow jobs for cigarettes. While the girls in the stories had different names and
nicknames, and while the rumors often varied in their
specifics, the myth of the promiscuous female remained constant. It was as reliable as an old wives' tale, as irrepressible as
a cliché. It was a story with a specific cadence, identifiable
themes, and a clear moral: Don't end up here. Don't end up in
the basement like she did.

I began to see that the promiscuous high school girl, isolated from the kids in the hallway, is actually part of a continuum. Bring her up among people who don't know one
another well, and instantly everyone finds themselves on
common ground. Bring her up at Thanksgiving dinner, and
people break out of their dull weather-talk. "Slut" is a word
everyone knows, a word that always provokes a response.
The word's provocative power and the continued vitality of
the myth behind the word imply that the slut is not a monster
but a sign: she's a window into the unconscious, a way of
deciphering how the culture dreams of women, even if we've
learned civilized people shouldn't have such dreams. Like
Dante's Virgil, she's the girl who can lead us into the underworld.

This book first took shape in the late 1990s. I was working for
an alternative weekly newspaper in Seattle, the kind of paper
that publishes calendar listings, left-leaning articles about
city politics, letters from revolutionary wackos. I had been
writing articles for several years about women-oriented topics, and I was racking my brain for my next idea.

It was fall, and I'd been having flashbacks of Anna Wanna. Each morning I drove past a big public high school on the way to work and saw kids hovering around one another, bright coats and voices cracking the air apart, like denizens of a parallel world that all of us in cars—all of us rush hour losers driving past—could only guess at.

I decided to research an article about a girl who is considered a high school slut, figuring it was a way of getting myself back inside the school's doors so many years later. One of the most read features in the paper was writer Dan Savage's sex column, "Savage Love." It was a raunchy, irreverent discussion of relationship and sex problems that, although written by a gay man, didn't cater specifically to either homosexuals or heterosexuals. It was part of a late-nineties blooming of no-holds-barred sexual discussion, of continuous chattering, twenty-four/seven, in on-line magazines, alternative weeklies, and the MTV chat show *Loveline*.

"Savage Love" had been syndicated in twenty cities when I placed a query there, asking for girls to call and tell me their stories. The query read: *Are you or were you the slut of your high school? Whether you earned the reputation or not, I would like to talk to you for an article I am writing. Confidentiality is guaranteed. Please call me or e-mail me.*

On the evening before the query was placed I activated an 800 number in my home. Readers who recognized themselves in my query could call free of charge and tell me their stories. I figured the free number would encourage girls and women to take the opportunity for a free confession, a chance to move the story of their lives a little further out into the open.

Within twenty-four hours, the phone started ringing. The reaction was swift and overwhelming. Within the space of two weeks I had received over ninety-five messages. By the time I had finished researching, I had talked and e-mailed with over 150 girls and women.

The constant ring of the phone took over the space of my office—an insistent chirp, another girl arriving out of the blue. After a while the ringing was so constant that I became accustomed to it; in fact, I was surprised by silence. Breaks occurred in the very early morning, or in the dead part of the afternoon, but for all intents and purposes the flow of confession was unstoppable, a river of messages:

"My whole past is a cesspool."

"My teenage years are like a violent porno."

"I can't believe this ever happened. It is so fucking unfair."

"I can't believe you are doing an article about this because I have become so, so angry about this very thing and I need to talk about it."

"According to the people I grew up with, I am the biggest whore in the world."

Here were the girls all of us had remembered that night at Thanksgiving dinner; here were the real, live women who had chafed beneath the myth. Ranging in age from thirteen to fifty-five, living in small towns, urban areas, or the same houses where they grew up, these women were by far the most dramatic, urgent, and adamant interview subjects I'd ever encountered as a journalist. They wanted to set the story straight, to put the rumors to rest, to calm the rage that the rumors ignited.

The conversations, letters, notes, and messages I exchanged with these women form the foundation of this book. Suspicious, angry, jokey, drunk, they were interactions that varied widely in their weight and emotional texture, that didn't often yield much insight or understanding, that didn't always come to any reliable conclusion. One girl told me, "You know, I realize I have got to stop talking to you. I need to get past this, and it is not good to talk about it." Seeking the story of the high school slut, I was often on the trail of a story that girls didn't want to waste their time on anymore. In order to get the girls to really open up I had to promise that I would change their names. "You will be anonymous. I'll change your school, your name, and no one will recognize you." It was the promise of anonymity that propelled many girls into their most profound and troubling confessions.

I supplemented in-person, phone, and e-mail interviews with reading and research. I figured that if the slut was a dream the culture was having, I needed to try to trace the dream in literary texts, feminist tracts, scientific studies, women's magazines, and old advertisements. By sifting through the evidence, I thought, I would learn more about how this story came to pass and why it refuses to release its grip. Contemporary feminist-oriented books on topics like sex and sexuality very often take the form of oral histories, but this is not a route I chose. Rather, the interviews and the voices of the girls took the form of threads, weaving and unweaving my various theories. The girls were my guides, but they were also guides I needed to leave behind eventually.

In the course of my research, a cluster of themes emerged that hinted toward a *type* who became the slut. Many of these girls experienced precocious puberty: breasts and hips when all the other girls were in training bras. Many had also experienced incest or some form of childhood sexual abuse, which resulted in the feeling of being a sexual freak or outcast. Many of them also revealed a tendency toward extroversion: they were not afraid of cussing someone out, talking dirty, or wearing short skirts to school. Often what many girls called "the whole slut thing" began when they departed from what seemed normal within the school's walls—for example, by transferring in, by being absent for a long period and then suddenly reappearing, by dyeing their hair a wild color.

Their narratives were so similar that at times I believed I knew what a girl was going to say before she said it. The feeling was exhilarating: one story opening up into another, a pattern emerging. And the girls themselves, convinced of their specificity and isolation, were often shocked to hear their story had been echoed by others. They'd never considered themselves part of a continuum, a sisterhood.

Over time I realized the stories sounded so similar in part because the America they were originating from was the same: small-town or suburban white America. Most of the girls who contacted me were rooted in this demographic; the slut story was not something that seemed to have an urban or multiracial backdrop. Instead it occurred largely among kids like the kind of kid I had been, kids who at the time of adolescence didn't have much knowledge of or exposure to the world outside the white American mainstream. The specific power arrangements of this America, and the language and myths kids learn there, delimited my generalizations and theories about what constitutes the slut experience.

Consequently, my conversations with girls who had not grown up in suburban white America tended to undermine what was constant in the slut story. Because I'd read my Foucault and learned that sex and sexuality have everything to do with the dynamics of power, I knew any generalization I made about crossing the threshold into sex and about the boundaries to the body would be destabilized by the experiences of nonwhite women, women who very often have a far different relationship with the basic elements of this story: name-calling, ostracism, the fight for identity itself. In chapter 9, I explore my experiences with the girls outside the limits of the main story, discussing the way their digressions and differences changed my project and made me see myself from the outside: a white girl from a white world.

Feminist theorists have argued that the real history of the world occurs in private spaces. It's an argument for illuminating the domestic sphere, but it's also an argument about the darkness of subjectivity: about how we can really never know one another, how we will always retreat into the isolation of the self at the end of the day. In my interviews, each girl carried with her a personal history. She carried it on her back like a shell, and her particularity, the lilt or tenor or whispery level of her voice, the way her eyes went in and out like lights—all these physical and physiological and psychological elements undermined my notions of a type, a theory that would always apply.

While I was well aware of the racial and class limits to our interactions, I also encountered limits to the self. I carried a temperament into the interview process, an emotional and spiritual tendency, a past. Like the boys in the back of the car, I was often looking for an answer from the mouth of a girl— an answer that would not upset my assumptions and that would allow me further and further inside. Inevitably I projected my own disposition onto the encounter. As a person who prefers sad songs and melodramatic movies, I gravitated toward the sad and melodramatic girls. It was not hard, given my subject matter, to find girls who appealed to my own need for drama. The ostracism they had endured or were still enduring often took on a hysterical and cruel edge and worked to drive the girls to desperate acts, so that a black wave of sadness rose up in our conversations rhythmically, fatefully, to the point where I started to anticipate it, perhaps even encouraging it to take form. Certainly I experienced some odd pleasure when the wave finally came.

Maybe all truths are emotional at their core; maybe every intellectual theory begins with something as irrational as a memory of a girl, one lost girl the mind can't shake. I know I couldn't come to any absolute truths here except the truths of memory and its power over the mind—the truth of flashbacks, moments when the past somehow seems unbearably and suddenly present, flashbacks of kids yelling in the hallway: *"Hey, slut! I heard what you did last weekend!"*

In sorting out my findings I avoided statistics or graphs, and I'm not proposing any prescriptions. Rather, I hope this book resides somewhere in the space between the kids who made the slut and the girls themselves; I hope to shed some light on that space in the high school hallway where so many vital and troubling encounters occur.

High school is both a microcosm and a distortion of the social world. The atmosphere of a school reflects the atmosphere of the town and the era in which it's situated. Perennial articles about our troubled teens are evidence of the way the adult world tries to read itself in kids, to see where we might have gone wrong and in which ways we might be threatened. How much trouble we believe the kids are in is a projection of our own anxiety, of our own feeling that the world might be coming apart. "How can we fix the kids?" television anchormen ask, but really the question is about deeper fears.

Many of the scenes in this book are based in a suburban Seattle high school whose name I have changed. I loitered there for a couple of weeks after getting permission from a good-hearted counselor. But when the administration heard about me taking notes in the cafeteria, they kicked me out. As I drove away that day, kicked out of school for the first time in my life, I wondered what it was they did not want me to see.

If high school is quintessentially modern, on the brink of every trend, it's also an ancient place full of impulses that seem to come from outside time. What happens among the kids in the hallways goes way, way back. Indeed, it seems as if it has been happening forever.

Like a tribe in an ancient forest telling stories about the moon, kids tell slut stories because they need an allegory for the mystery of sex itself—a mystery that lives outside language, that causes numerous storms in the blood, that rips the lining from the mind. In the 1991 film *My Own Private Idaho*, director Gus Van Sant likened the turning point of orgasm to an image of a barn falling from the sky, crashing to pieces on a deserted highway. It was a beautifully futile attempt to represent an overwhelming physical sensation on-screen.

As adolescents' bodies flood with hormones, rumors become something for them to hold on to. The wordless, crashing power of sex makes teenagers want to name it, control it, find a pattern for it. The slut becomes a way for the adolescent mind to draw a map. She's the place on the map marked by a danger sign, where legions of boys have been lost at sea. She's the place where a girl should never wander, for fear of becoming an outcast.

Watching Anna in the hallways at Washington when I was a teenager, I could feel the whole churning world of sex knocking against my mind, racking my nerves. I was afraid of what might happen if I gave in, if I moved beyond crushes and teen idols to the realm of nakedness and furious pleasure. I was afraid of sex the same way I was afraid of blackouts, snakes, life itself. So I stood back, sweating in my new shoes. I practiced hard on the piano. I stayed on the map and wasn't a worry to anyone. Looking back, I often wish I had worried someone, at least worried myself. Often I wish I'd had the courage to cross the hall and talk to Anna, to ask her to tell her story. Maybe now, so long after the fact, that is what I'm doing here.

To pin a girl down with a name like "slut," "whore," "skank" is an archaic, irrational compulsion. The desire to name girls and thereby tame them within the garden of the world goes all the way back to Adam. He walked through the garden naming the trees and the beasts, placing all the flying and crawling creatures into categories, pinning the world down with language so it would no longer escape his grasp. He did this in the midst of a million disasters: as Eve came out of his rib and then disappeared with a whispering snake. He named the world not out of love but out of panic.

Although high school is about as far away from the Garden of Eden as you can get, still, in those hallways this urge continues: to name and to grasp one another, to pin one another down as types, as species, as haves and have-nots, as you look warily around at the lush, foreign place in which you find yourself, trying to figure out how to live among these strangers without being exiled.

1

HIGH SCHOOL'S SECRET LIFE

All domination takes the form of
administration.

–Herbert Marcuse, *Eros and Civilization*

People have been afraid of teenagers for a long time. The way
they moon around in perpetual lovesickness, the way they
threaten to erase themselves from the picture—die from
drugs, permanently defy curfew, wrap their cars around telephone poles. Society fears teenagers because of the chaotic
element they represent: the point after the law of the father
has started to wear off but before the law of the land has been
internalized. It is a period when everything is being questioned and everything is up for grabs—a moment of limbo
during which anything could happen.

Teenagers disrupt the order of the home by suddenly

locking doors, locking diaries, hiding under layers of clothes, demanding privacy with their erupting bodies. The invasion of hormones turns the child into a stranger, and the stranger in the house forces adults to ask questions: What happens behind the closed door? What dreams live behind the half-closed eyes? What does the body need, and furthermore, why does the body suddenly seem so urgent, angry, maybe transgressively beautiful?

In developmental terms, teen restlessness is called *sexual awakening,* as if before the moment of adolescence kids were asleep but now they live in a psychological morning, disorienting in its brightness. While the awakening is sexual and hormonal, it's also total: a shift in the mind, rounding a corner in the imagination, coming to a place where you are neither a child nor an adult, a psychological juncture where you can no longer see or understand the person you were, but neither can you see the person you might become. It is a crossroads where many kids realize that theirs is not the only town in the world, that lies were perhaps being told in the family, that fears were being propagated and secrets were being preserved in the basement.

The drama and innocence of awakening is the allure of coming-of-age tales. The fascination that teenagers inspire in the collective imagination has been revealed in magazine features about "our troubled adolescents," exploited on porn sites advertising "lusty teens," funded by grant committees trying to get to the bottom of the whole youth problem. In 1990, writer Donna Gaines explored the third-world country of teenagedom in her book *Teenage Wasteland.* After a group of four sixteen-year-old friends committed suicide in the small town of Bergenfield, New Jersey, Gaines traveled to the town in an attempt to find out how this tragedy had come about, what dark visions could have compelled the kids to such extreme hopelessness. With spooky persuasiveness, Gaines argued that the actions of teenagers might be prophetic, and their self-annihilation might carry ominous signs about the future of the world: "When I heard about the suicide pact it grabbed me in the solar plexus. I looked at the pictures of the kids and their friends. I read what the reporters said. I was sitting in my garden apartment looking out on Long Island's Jericho Turnpike thinking maybe this is how the world ends, with the last generation bowing out first."

Gaines moved among the teenagers of Bergenfield for many months, becoming part of their crew. Sometimes they'd lift up their sleeves and show her the scars on their wrists. In one passage she wrote about the state of "burnout," which is a way of "slipping out the back door with the body still present." She observed that for the burned-out kids she had met in Bergenfield, sometimes it took everything just to keep the soul from taking leave of the body altogether. If certain moments of pain become unrelenting and acute enough, Gaines showed, kids might decide to take themselves out of the game permanently—cutting their arms open, blowing their brains out, lying back in a Camaro in a closed garage until their hearts stop.

When Gaines talked about the soul slipping out the back door, she evoked the restless teen crawling out windows in the middle of the night. The moment wherein they seem to take leave of us while still in our midst lies at the root of our fear of teenagers. We can't help but wonder: What would they tell us if they resisted the need to slip out the window? What would they tell us if they were really here? What would they tell us if they ever really came home?

Faced with self-destructive kids, high school counselors and administrators counterattack in various ways. In American public schools, a series of self-improvement programs are administered each year: after-school clubs to keep kids out of trouble, antidrug and antiviolence assemblies where horror stories of addiction and reckless driving are recounted as a way of warning kids about consequences. Walk through the hallways of virtually any high school and you will see walls plastered with information about what to do if you find yourself in crisis, and how to avoid the crisis once you detect it looming on the horizon.

In high school counseling centers, the overwhelming sense of crisis has been organized and separated into three main categories: drugs, sex, and violence. In counseling terms, drugs, sex, and violence are perceived as the three enemies of the ideal teenager; they are the three forces that threaten to pull kids out of the light into the darkness. Call it the drugs-sex-violence trinity: it works to reduce the dangerousness of the world by locating the sources of danger and placing danger into categories, lists, catalogues of warning signs.

The drugs-sex-violence pamphlets locate the threat to teenagers' well-being in elements that enter the body from the outside: teenagers come into the world and the school pure, but then they are threatened by nefarious influences such as rap music, guns, pot, sexual pressure. This logic assumes a certain original innocence, which the outside world steals from the teenager. But does the world make the teenager, or the teenager make the world? Warning them against the dangers of their environment, adults turn teenagers back into children easily scared by cautionary tales. But they will never be children again. Neither children nor adults, teenagers are beings from a frontier of morality that can be a ruthless and unsettling place. The drugs-sex-violence campaign is a battle for a kind of spiritual dominance over this frontier, an attempt to exert some semblance of control over the uncontrollable future that teenagers embody, to exert some rule over the tribes.

In 1999 a warning pamphlet was circulated through public high schools. Called *The Marijuana Addict, at a Glance*, it's a remarkable piece of administrative prose that reveals a lot about the debased and contradictory ways America addresses its teenagers.

The Marijuana Addict AT A GLANCE
WHAT THEY THINK THEY ARE vs. WHAT THEY ARE

Believe they have good personal insight and awareness.	Are out of touch and deluded; live in a dream world.
Believe that success, fame, and fortune are just a matter of time.	Have grandiose illusions which have little chance of becoming reality.
Believe they have control of their lives in most areas.	Have little control because they are out of touch with reality, their thinking is impaired, they procrastinate, they are paranoid.

After puzzling over this pamphlet repeatedly, I finally realized the irony. The marijuana addict being described and dissected (after being "glanced" at) was not much different from a dyed-in-the-wool American dreamer, the kind of man we learned about in social studies class who walked two miles through the snow to school and believed "that success, fame, and fortune are just a matter of time." And while the pamphlet recognizes "living in a dream world" as a sign of deviance, the same kids who are being warned against the dream's dangers are reading *The Great Gatsby* in freshman lit. In Fitzgerald's irresistible perception, no matter how pathetic the dreamer becomes, he still possesses a glamorous beauty, a beauty ripe for idolatry and imitation.

The essential problem with most of the language confronting teenagers in the name of help is its refusal to recognize the irresistible and often destructive beauty of the dreamworld. Counseling-center language is a gray language of obligation and forced cheerfulness, encouraging kids to "Try random acts of kindness!" or "Look on the sunny side of life!" While many admirable and life-changing high school teachers and counselors reach the kids despite the clichés and the goofy pamphlets, the terms themselves—the terms in which the argument has been set—long ago lost their currency, if they ever had any currency at all.

One of the most perennial deterrent assemblies presented in American high schools is the car crash assembly. Every year around prom, a mangled car is brought before an auditorium or gym full of kids, and a policeman or paramedic gives a tour of the shell of a car in which real kids died—kids who drank too much and followed their self-destructive impulses to their terrible conclusion. Teaching the lessons of careless- ness, the man points to the various areas of the car, some- times showing graphic footage of bodies or film of the Jaws of Life. He might talk about the velocity at which the doomed kids hit the windshield. He might try to describe the excruci- ating pain of the broken back or the broken neck. All of this is meant, of course, as a warning, a deterrent.

Nevertheless, no matter how many times they stare into the Jaws of Life, a significant number of kids will still want to pursue the wrecked world, get totally wasted or obliterated, immerse themselves in their own vanishing. Teenagers con- tinue to create full-blown nihilistic evenings despite the warnings, and the persistence of their self-destructive desire is a testament to the way the power of this call cannot be pre- dicted or eradicated. Maybe it's one of those mysteries that can't be solved. The desire to feel the rush for yourself—this desire can't be underestimated.

Calhoun High is located on the outskirts of Seattle, Washing- ton. A school with a population consisting of mostly working- class white kids, it's located near the freeway. From the Calhoun parking lot, you can hear the traffic, constant as breathing. In 1999, Seattle is a booming new-rich economy, and Calhoun has recently erected a new school building: shiny and modern, with wheelchair ramps and automatic doors, a computer lab with state-of-the-art equipment. The building is so new it seems to have no ghosts. Walls are made of materials such that the moment graffiti is written, it can be washed away.

I spend a series of mornings loitering in the Calhoun cafeteria, observing the tribes of this particular high school. The smell of heat-lamp food, the overhead fluorescent lights, the lunch ladies in their hair nets—all of it brings up my own past in the Washington High cafeteria, where I looked around furtively, trying to find my two friends. Sitting on the sidelines now, I can still feel the adolescent loneliness in my guts.

The cafeteria is high school's proving ground. It's one of the most unavoidable and important thresholds, the place where you find out if you have friends or if you don't. The cafeteria is the place where forms of human sacrifice occur, the merciless rituals of cruelty on which the kids thrive.

Although Calhoun's new building was supposed to be big enough for all of the kids, it seems that more and more of them keep coming out of the woodwork. Because of overcrowding, lunch happens in three shifts: ten-thirty, eleven-fifteen, and noon. Kids who've drawn first lunch often don't seem very hungry—they're wiping the sleep from their eyes and panicking about forgotten homework. They drink coffee, hunched over like harried executives. All the special ed kids are assigned to first lunch. During second lunch, the pace picks up, but the luckiest kids have third lunch, the "fun" lunch.

Each group of kids moves in and out quickly, and in the brief interludes of emptiness, custodians move through with giant brooms. Every time they migrate, the kids leave items behind: backpacks, notebooks, jackets, eyeglasses.

If the cafeteria is the place where kids experience the most prolonged moments of relative freedom, it's also the place where they experience an unobstructed nearness. In these free moments, violence can erupt, and Calhoun has employed an armed cafeteria monitor, a nice guy in a golf shirt with a gun tucked discreetly into his belt.

As the school's ground zero, the cafeteria's tension derives from the way the kids are both in and out of school. It's a decentered environment, a place where they can make independent choices: sit where they want to sit, whisper to their friends whom they are separated from in class.

Cafeteria life at Calhoun is a game of chance: devastation comes when a kid draws the wrong lunch. One girl tells me about how she used to feel like she had friends, but then all her friends were assigned to third lunch and she was stuck in second by herself. The second-lunch destiny changed her idea of herself as a girl with friends. Now she sees her crowd only after school, and there are many stories she never hears, many plans she is left out of. She tries not to be bitter when she talks to me, but she's clearly troubled that there's no way to cross over into the third-lunch realm now, a realm as distant as the Emerald City.

This girl hovers somewhere on the edge of a tribe; she's not a complete outcast but she isn't popular either. She's arty and bohemian, she possesses a complex prettiness that boys will probably notice later. Although she is clearly in a bind, stuck without her friends, her loneliness is relatively manageable and escapable. Other kids operate on a deeper level of loneliness: an obese girl valiantly ignores the snickers of the boys across the aisle from her as she eats during first lunch; a boy at second lunch has some strange muscle condition that causes him to swat the air, as if he's surrounded by insects.

No matter whether it's first, second, or third lunch, the popular kids always cluster around the same geographical area of the cafeteria: in the front, near the windows. The popular kids sit so close together sometimes they can barely move, smashed into one or two long tables, often remaining on the benches out of sheer will and masterful balance. This is what it means to be part of a crowd: to always have people jammed next to you on the cafeteria bench.

At Calhoun, virtually all the popular kids are physically well proportioned; one girl I interview will later describe them as "the kind of kids who get their way because they have perfect hair, perfect teeth, et cetera." Their conformity is remarkable: in haircuts, necklaces, the way they slouch, the way they use their voices. They all imitate one another because the imitation speaks of their power. In this context, conformity is not a cop-out but a way of broadcasting the fact that you aren't a weirdo, that you are speaking in the signs of the chosen ones.

The popular kids at Calhoun dress in the ubiquitous trendy brand Abercrombie & Fitch. They sport the logo on T-shirts, pants, bags, baseball hats. Calhoun is a school that emphasizes athletics, and Abercrombie & Fitch is a clothing line advertised by soccer-playing boys with perfect tanned bodies and sleek girl models with Grace Kelly class. The mystique of the brand is very East Coast, Kennedy clan, Martha's Vineyard, prep school. In other words, it has nothing to do with the working-class history of Calhoun, where most kids end up going to a local college and never grow up to drink Bloody Marys on Sundays in the Hamptons.

Between the extremes of the popular kids and the loners, there's a vast middle region. The tribes within this region are numerous. A group of overgrown Girl Scouts called the "natural helpers" are neither popular nor outcast; they are girls who are always busy doing charity work, committing an extreme number of good deeds. There are theater kids, who sit near the back of the cavernous space, immersed in the news of the next play, good at acting confident, always an edge of an act about them, always making entrances and exits. There are the computer geniuses, at Calhoun all of them unwashed, disheveled boys; they never seem to look in mirrors or out the window at the natural world. The screens of their computers take their eyes away from everything. A boy carefully pops open his laptop as he devours the cafeteria's fluorescent orange nachos, careful not to drip on his keyboard.

One of the most notable groups in the Calhoun cafeteria appears during third lunch: a gang of boys, huge but not athletic, class clowns, druggies, and rock and rollers. They possess a screaming, ballistic life drive and although they seem to differ in matters of style, their formidable restlessness—their energy of trouble—holds them together. From the moment they enter the cafeteria, the man with the gun hovers around them. Even when I am sitting on the opposite end of the room, I can hear them going wild. Even in my position as an invisible extra to the drama, trying to disappear into the background, I am a little afraid of them, of where their energy might settle, of what might happen if it settles in the wrong place.

This particular week has been designated Multicultural Week. It's a time when kids are encouraged to look up from their lunches and recognize the larger world. Posters advertise, *Celebrate Diversity!* The multiculturalism club is putting on an around-the-world potluck. One day a lone, red-faced girl dances a Scottish jig in the cafeteria, celebrating her heritage, jumping around diligently to a scratchy tape of bagpipes. The spectacle of the girl displaying herself before everyone silences the tribes and lowers the volume of each conversation. For a moment, as she begins her strange dance, there's only a flabbergasted stillness.

Some days messengers travel from tribe to tribe, proving that webs can be formed even if they are fragile and fleeting. One day I watch the natural helpers moving from table to table, collecting money for the "penny wars." The idea is that if everyone contributes a penny, all the pennies will be given to the local homeless shelter. In the name of the penny wars, these girls reach out to the other kids in the cafeteria with a slightly condescending smile; with their jars held out, they cross the boundaries of the tribes. It is interesting to watch the rush of this moment, when boundaries are crossed and the lonely kids are being addressed, even if it's only a plea for pennies. The computer geeks look up at the natural helpers as if they are angels. The rowdy boys, the fat girl, the boy swatting the air, the arty girls, the pale orchestra kids, the boy with a T-shirt that reads PORN STAR—they all are amazed that these natural helpers suddenly stand in front of them. "Give a penny for the penny wars!" the helpers say, beaming like saints.

*   *   *

The cover of the May 3, 1999, issue of *Time* magazine asked: THE MONSTERS NEXT DOOR, WHAT MADE THEM DO IT? Eric Harris and Dylan Klebold were high school juniors at Columbine High in Littleton, Colorado. They were minor juvenile offenders into role-playing games like Dungeons & Dragons, outcast boys labeled as geeks who nevertheless had enough of an identity and presence to gain a reputation as the Trenchcoat Mafia. On April 20 at approximately 11:15 A.M., they entered Columbine High School armed with semiautomatic weapons and hand grenades; they had already planted bombs all over the school. They opened fire in the school hallways; when they were finished, they had killed thirteen kids and seriously wounded dozens more. They had also killed themselves.

The Columbine story was captured in live news footage— cops surrounding the perimeter, kids running out in pairs, dragging one another out of windows, jumping carelessly from high ledges. The siege lasted for over four hours. Every major TV and radio news outlet interrupted regular broadcasting to run the story. While shootings had happened before in American high schools, Columbine was the bloodiest. And Columbine happened on the wall-to-wall news channels of cable television.

Maybe events need to happen on television before they can truly activate the modern collective mind. What happened after Columbine seemed at times like a societal nervous breakdown. The country was spooked and transformed. Monsters were everywhere. Hundreds of high schools banned the wearing of trench coats altogether, for fear that the kids wearing them were part of a nationwide Trenchcoat

Mafia. Bomb scares centered on left-behind lunch bags or laptop computers.

Columbine briefly illuminated high school's tribal world, its primitivism, its phenomenal danger, the destructive darkness that the counseling center tries to counter with its cheerful slogans. Since the shooters targeted jocks and popular kids, these favored sons and daughters were suddenly perceived as endangered, as the focus of homicidal rage, no longer merely the darlings of cheering crowds at football games. Columbine hysteria was a uniquely white, suburban phenomenon: while urban schools had long ago installed metal detectors, there was still an overarching and subtly racist belief that suburbia was safe from gun violence.

It was a surreal moment in America and a strange time to be loitering around Calhoun. By the time I found myself there, the hysteria had worn off a little, but trench coats were still banned. Looking around, trying to see which kids the faculty might single out as "Columbine kids," I focused on the crazy boys at third lunch. They came closest to fitting the Columbine stereotype: they had an air of neglect, trouble, and war about them. Were they *the ones*?

This is the conspiratorial train of thought unleashed by the Columbine massacre: the fear of a vengeful adolescent uprising we didn't see coming, fueled by nihilistic hatred and an endless supply of firearms; the belief that teenagers are messed-up psychopaths; the belief that our lumbering American boys have turned into monsters from video games.

*   *   *

In the Calhoun principal's office, the secretaries wonder if "it" will ever happen to them. The secretaries are ladies in sensible skirts and tennis shoes who seem to know every teacher, student, and substitute by first name. All day long they share snacks and gossip about faculty members; they fill out forms that hold the civilization of the school together; they send out schedules to tell kids where they should be and when.

One afternoon the secretaries talk about the possibility of their own destruction at the hands of armed students. "You know, I was thinking about it last night," the head secretary, a woman with the husky voice of a chain-smoker, says. "We're sitting ducks here. I was thinking, what would I do if they came in shooting? Could I fit under here?" She points to the small cave beneath her desk.

"I don't know, I think I would just run for it," says another. "I mean, the door is close enough. If you heard shooting, maybe if you were quick enough you could get outside."

The secretaries talk like people living in a war zone; a pageant of violence is always ready to unfold in their imaginations and scare the daylights out of them. While these women are supposed to play a maternal role in the life of the school— asking kids, "What's wrong, honey?" when they come into the administration office—in the wake of Columbine they've begun to imagine themselves as targets, wondering aloud if they should erect a wall of bulletproof glass.

Yet the secretaries aren't afraid of all the kids; rather, they're afraid of a certain type, a certain tribe, the trench coat wearers and video game players. They hope to be able to recognize this tribe "at a glance." They want to recognize the unsafe kids, the kids who should be frisked before they're allowed inside.

*   *   *

Thus for a brief moment in America, the horde of students and the adults who tried to administer to them huddled close together, united against a common enemy. Everyone felt threatened by the same monsters. One girl told me, "I think since then, people are being a little nicer to each other. You know, like it could have been us, and it makes us appreciate each other more." Nevertheless, eventually Columbine horror stories were replaced by feel-good Columbine hero stories, and the news crews returned to wars in other countries or political scandals in Washington. The secretaries cooled off and returned to family and faculty gossip. The popular kids regained their swaggering confidence. In the hallways the talk was no longer about killers and bombs; it was about other forms of monstrousness and more subtle forms of erasure: who is a "fag," who is a "lesbo," who is a "psycho," who is a *slut*.

2

THE GIRL IN THE RUMOR

"They say the devil is whispering in your ear."
"I cannot help it if they do say it."

—Transcript of the trial of Dorcas Hoar,
convicted of witchcraft in 1871

It's the day of the big pep assembly at Calhoun High. Teachers corral the kids into the gym, admonishing, "Hustle, people, hustle. No playing around!" Bleachers unfold to the rafters; kids take the steps two at a time. Slowly the shining metal skeleton of bleachers is covered with shifting bodies. The bleachers are tree branches, the kids are gathering birds. The gym's light is flat and much too bright. Sneakers screech on varnished wood. Twittery, sugar-high cheerleaders practice their routines.

On the far wall of the gym the school fight song is posted:

> *Victory, victory for Calhoun High!*
> *Our pride and honor reach the sky!*
> *Win, win, win and never rest!*
> *Calhoun High is the best!*

The school-spirit banner looks like it was just pulled out of a dusty closet—faded red-and-white felt, a crust of dirt forming around the edges. It's a meaningless and forgotten bit of encouragement, like the cheerful *Hang In There!* posters on the wall of the counseling center. These sunny truisms and cadences fade into the background of the school's life like elevator music.

The idea behind school spirit goes something like this: if you feel the school is something you are proud of, something you're "true" to, then you will feel like a winner all around. The banner at Calhoun High advertises the hollow and hegemonic peppiness that many remember long after high school as a fantastic example of disingenuousness. In the late 1990s a series of horror movies, most notably *The Faculty*, played on the idea of school spirit as an evil, alien language and attitude. In this particular movie, the football team, the cheerleaders, all the be-true-to-your-school fanatics, were actually invaders from a hostile planet.

School-spirit language rings false mostly because high school is such a clear spectacle of cruelty. Clearly the school has no one truth, no abiding or benevolent spirit. The evidence is all around me as I sit in the bleachers at the pep assembly. I'm next to a clutch of girls who keep straining their necks trying to flirt with the jocks in the row behind us, muscular boys buff from sports practice, wearing team jerseys with their names on the back. These boys are always moving, slapping one another, pulling one another's hat off, flicking spitballs. The girls next to me are hyperaware of them and desperate to get a look, a glance, a moment in their radar.

The assembly features the candidates for various student government positions. The kids campaigning to win have postered the school: VOTE FOR NORM FOR REFORM. ANNE BEST IS THE BEST. Today's the day they make their campaign speeches. "Vote for me, I'm Paul D.," a geeky white boy chants, rapping against the backdrop of a drum machine. He promises longer lunches and more money for dances. He's unfazed by the huge crowd and by the deep-voiced boy in the back row yelling repeatedly: "You are a fag!"

Just as Paul D. finishes his campaign pitch, in the short dead space between candidates, a rumor begins, a rumor about a girl I'll call Heather Adams.

The rumor goes like this: *Heather Adams masturbates. Pass it on!*

The rumor begins among the jocks behind me. Soon it has been heard by a dozen kids or more. *Pass it on, pass it on.* Over and over the phrase is repeated, cupped hands touching ears, the whisper as loud as a stage whisper: *"Heather Adams masturbates. Pass it on!"*

"Gross!" says the female recipient of this news, a red-faced beanpole. She hesitates for a moment, then whispers the news into the ear of the girl sitting in front of her. "Are you kidding?" the girl shouts. "She is sooo sick!"

The rumor moves west through the crowd. The point of the rumor, its defining quality, is that it moves. The rumor can't stop. It's a hot rock that must be passed quickly before it begins to burn.

While down below, in the middle of the basketball court, the student council candidates make a variety of optimistic campaign promises about dances and athletic budgets and the great history of Calhoun High, up here in the bleachers, sitting side by side and influenced by one another's skin and smell and possibility, the kids stop hearing the messages and promises of school-spirit language. They do not care about the future or about the school's phony history. They care about the present. They care about what it feels like to be sitting so near to one another. The nearness is almost unbearable. They are dying for a reaction, and they have found a phrase sure to create one: *Heather Adams masturbates.*

A 1963 book called *Improvised News: A Sociological Study of Rumor* attempted a quasi-scientific exploration of how rumors work. Writer Tamotsu Shibutani explained that a rumor "is a message transmitted by word of mouth from person to person. Indeed, oral interchange is frequently regarded as *the* identifying characteristic of rumor. Whereas news in print is fixed, in oral transmission some transformation is inevitable, for only a few can remember a complicated message verbatim."

Through documents and stories from various historical periods when rumors seemed to flourish—during the McCarthy era, among civilian populations during wartime, among soldiers in the midst of battle—Shibutani attempted to find out why some stories flourish, flowering into rumors, while others don't travel far out of the circle where they've originated. He wanted to get to the bottom of this strange, hysterical tendency of human societies.

Shibutani's book is not widely printed or read anymore; it's a dated volume, earnest in its objectivity, that does not incorporate postmodern theories, which always admit to some subjectivity on the part of the author. Nevertheless, *Improvised News* is illuminating on the subject of the rumor's context. Although it's a book that never addresses teenagers, the contexts Shibutani describes as ideal for rumor from his studies of various populations sound a lot like descriptions of high school. "Rumors thrive among populations desperately trying to comprehend their environment," Shibutani writes. Rumors "flourish in periods of sudden crises, sustained tension, impending decisions, boredom from monotony."

All Shibutani's elements are overwhelmingly present in high school. The author could have been writing from the interior of a cafeteria. Like the populations *Improvised News* analyzed, high school kids spread rumors to alleviate the sense of crisis and the atmosphere of monotony. Clustered together on the bleachers or crammed onto the cafeteria benches, kids are perched in an in-between state, neither here nor there, and all they can do is succumb to deep compulsions of exaggerated storytelling. The stories are vessels that rescue them from the sea of confusion.

As the pep assembly drags on, the "Heather Adams masturbates" rumor drifts from kid to kid. The story they are telling about Heather Adams is perhaps the most private story possible. It's a story that hinges on the idea that a girl pleasuring herself is scandalous. The way the kids react, full of gusto and outrage, indicates that even thirty years after the sexual revolution, the idea of women masturbating is still taboo. Even in the post-Madonna American high school, the notion of Heather Adams and her gross pleasures shocks the kids who hear the rumor.

The word itself, "masturbate," qualifies as a dirty word. Watching the rumor and its effect, I remember my mother asking me and my sisters, "Are you talking dirty?" (Inevitably, she always knew when we were.) Other warnings: Don't be dirty minded. Get your mind out of the gutter. Yet the dirty mind keeps reemerging, and in high school the dirty mind— the desire to gross one another out, to talk about the extremes of the body—is arguably the mind that rules the school. It's the one great constant, the true school spirit.

In the theater of the dirty mind, Heather Adams is the temporary star. I don't know if Heather Adams is the slut of Calhoun High. But I know the way the kids are talking about her resembles the way kids talked about the girls I interviewed; they are simultaneously aroused and disgusted by her sexuality. The reaction to her is visceral, physical. She gets all the way under the skin.

Like a landscape transformed by fire, a girl's life can be swiftly transformed by rumor. The whole attitude of the hallway can change in an instant. "All of a sudden people are looking at you and you wonder, is there toilet paper on my shoe?"

explains Sasha, a twenty-eight-year-old who attended a small East Coast boarding school. Her reputation began forming over a three-day weekend, and by Tuesday she was the focus of an unfamiliar energy. "In a small school it's not like you can lose yourself," she says. "So I just stayed there, on the receiving end of all this bizarre stuff." Another girl, who was called Missile Tits because of her large breasts, remembers how she felt caught in a "bizarre web of repression," unable to move or change, unable to progress. Throughout my interviews I heard stories of how the rumors would build around a girl, getting thicker and thicker, like a chrysalis. The girls would try to disassociate themselves from the stories but they would find they could not move out from under the rumor's influence.

Generally the girls I interviewed were most impressed by the rumor's swiftness, its strange efficiency. One day they were part of the crowd; the next day they were the crowd's target. This transformation happens quickly and it happens outside the realm of adult supervision. Like my mother warning my sisters and me against talking dirty, the conventional role of the adult is to tell kids, "Don't talk that way," and then close the door. Once teenagers' talk becomes graphic, adults reflexively pull away from the posture of listening and close themselves off. Outside the radar of supervision, set adrift with a series of last-minute warnings, the kids talk trash amongst themselves. The rumors spread effortlessly. The girl becomes more and more a figment of the imagination. In the clouded atmosphere of the collective dirty mind, the slut takes on a sheen of unreality. She's not really a girl, she's more like a hallucination.

*   *   *

Madeline is a twenty-five-year-old Calhoun High graduate. She's the reason I chose this school to infiltrate. Even though she attended classes in the old school building that was later demolished, the way she says the name Calhoun High—the bitter sarcasm in her voice, the apparent volume of her rage—eventually makes me want to go out and see it for myself. When Madeline talks about her years there, I realize how much power one small building can have, how it houses certain experiences that brand themselves in the memory, so that even after the structure of the building is demolished, the structure of its experiences still exists.

Madeline is a voluptuous, dark-eyed girl with a theatrical persona—the kind of person who looks like she could make a big pronouncement at any time, or ruin a dinner party. She exudes a complex and troubled energy, seems all wound up by grief, believes the world owes her something. She says of being the slut of Calhoun, "It really pisses me off when I start to wonder, why did this happen to me?"

The rumors about Madeline were various: She had crabs, AIDS, herpes. She liked to suck dick. She was a lesbian. She moonlighted as a prostitute. "I had books thrown at me. People wrote WHORE on my locker in lipstick. They left a bottle of RID in front of my locker. One time I was at the mall and a bunch of girls came up to me and started shoving me. This girl I had never seen in my life was shoving me and calling me a slut." Once a group of girls beat her up in the driveway of a party, grinding the side of her face into the pavement.

Madeline identified a period before she was branded the

slut, when the world seemed to open out before her, when she felt at home and at peace. "As a kid I was really happy. I rode horses," Madeline said. "Then I somehow got completely screwed up."

Once, she and her mother took a trip to Ireland to meet their relatives. Her Irish grandmother warned her, "Don't write in red pen or you will become a whore." The fear of becoming a whore was prevalent among the women in her family; it was a destiny they often commented on and warned Madeline about.

By the time she entered high school, Madeline's mother had married a "major asshole," and Madeline's body had started to betray her. The period when she was happy and rode horses darkened, narrowed to the size of a scene watched through a keyhole. She was fourteen but her breasts belonged to the body of a woman: size 36D. The kids in the hallway stared, talked loudly about her "big tits." At twenty-five, looking back, she realizes she must have looked like "a goddess, only a hundred and twenty-five pounds." But to the kids she wasn't a goddess; she was a monster.

The kids weren't the only ones who gossiped about her; the faculty thought Madeline was trouble, too. She dressed provocatively and strutted into class late. She hung out with smokers. Once a teacher stopped her in front of everyone and said, "Go home and put some clothes on, young woman." Faculty, other students, girlfriends—everyone agreed Madeline was asking for it.

At home her stepdad tried to rape her. They were alone in the house and she fought him off. When she told her brother about it he simply said, "What do you expect, walking around the house in your nightgown?" Like the teacher in school, her brother equated Madeline's visual presence with all the abuse she'd been getting; he talked as if she should be punished for the way she looked. If she dressed a certain way, these things were going to happen to her, her life was going to take a certain course. It was only a matter of time.

All the contradictions and injustices started to revolve in her brain much too fast. She smoked pot, and pot slowed things down a little, but not enough. She was part of the stoner culture, which at Calhoun High meant "fishnet stockings, cutoffs, heavy metal concert T-shirts." Yet although on the surface she was part of a group of friends, girls within the group started to look at her warily, checking out her breasts, her eyes, her hair. They perceived something slutty about her, some bad energy.

"All of us girls, the clothes we wore were provocative. So I presented this image, but every single one of my girlfriends dressed the same way. I had a hard time figuring out why I was singled out when all of my friends had been sleeping with other people and I was the one that wasn't."

Guarding their men against her nefarious influence, the other stoner girls would call Madeline at home, two or three girls on the line at once, whispering, "You stay away from our boyfriends or we're gonna kick your ass." These whispery threats on the other end of the phone, and Madeline's stepdad in the next room, full of beer—it all added up to "a bad scene. I couldn't go anywhere or do anything," she says. "There was nothing I could do to stop any of it."

*　　　*　　　*

Madeline had been chosen as a type by the kids around her, a type that was part of the American sexual imagination, part of the world they were born into. In 1967, *The Seventeen Guide to Knowing Yourself* succinctly described the fast girl as "someone who is using sex to work out problems that have little to do with sex; and her solution only creates deeper problems. . . . It is a fact that most boys lose respect for an 'easy mark' and after a torrid affair are quite likely to decide that the young woman is 'not the kind of girl I want to be the mother of my children.'"

The idea expressed in this passage is an age-old cliché about a promiscuous woman's sexual cheapness, an idea integral to the high school slut experience. Just as married women often describe themselves as "off the market," so too the metaphors of the marketplace attach themselves to the slut girl's sense of herself. The girls I interviewed often felt that by being the slut they had been devalued; they would no longer have currency in the love-story economy and consequently they would never be allowed the redemption of romantic love.

Now in her twenties, Madeline has carried into adulthood the feeling of cheapness evoked by the slut story. She described the way she never felt like she belonged in "classy places"; for example, when she was in a nice restaurant one night and saw someone from high school, "all those worthless feelings came back." Other girls talked around this notion of worthlessness, of a decline in value brought on by being the center of the rumor mill.

Women confessed that they were not sure if a guy would want to spend much time with them once he knew the whole story of the slut years. For these women the sordid past does not have to do with sexual partners or sexual acts committed so much as it has to do with the bizarre experience of being the focus of the rumor mill—the unforgettable experience of being constantly talked about in sexually explicit terms. Being a slut is not about the body so much as all the things that have been spoken about the body. In my interviews I talked to some girls who had actually been promiscuous, some girls who hadn't. Some girls were virgins; one girl had slept with seventy men in the space of her high school years. But in the mind of the crowd, all of these girls had slept with "everyone."

When Madeline talked about her fourteen-year-old, 36D body and the way kids reacted to it, as if her body meant something about the things she would do, she was echoing the stories of many of the girls I interviewed. Girls who experienced bad reputations tended to be under the spell of what physicians call precocious puberty, a state of development when the body is moving ahead of time, hasty and accelerated.

"I had hips and underwire bras when I was twelve," says Andrea, who grew up in Orange County. "My boobs were huge," says Jenny, an East Coast tattoo artist. "The kids just called me Big." Other breast-related nicknames I heard included the aforementioned Missile Tits, Dolly Parton, Stacks, Big Rack. These names might be shouted out of car windows, blurted out in prank calls, or chanted by a group of boys in the middle of the cafeteria.

Twenty-two-year-old Tricia tells the story of how her overdeveloped breasts brought on all forms of crisis. At ten years old she had the body of a woman, and the boys thought this meant she *was* one, somehow, and that she was a woman meant for them. "My brother had a lot of friends, and they would come over to our house, and whenever they would see me they would chase after me. When I was ten, that was the first time I experienced washing cum out of my hair," she says. One night, her brother's friends became so hot and bothered they chased her out into the street and up into a huge oak tree that bordered the family's property. She climbed up there like a cat. "I can't believe I've been trapped in trees before. And I almost got raped two or three times. We'd be playing games at night and they'd trap me in corners."

Trapped in a corner with her erupting body, Tricia could not fathom why these boys wanted to touch her so desperately. Her experience is an example of the way the girl who is experiencing precocious puberty endures a split at adolescence far more intense than the conventional split of moody teenage alienation, the split between childhood and adulthood. For these girls, the split is literal: Her body begins to demolish and erase her interior life. Her body becomes the focus of a kind of visceral attention, a fiery need.

In this way, the girl who develops ahead of time feels like she is being pulled forward, suddenly thrust into the harsh light of the world's gaze. To awaken into the body of a woman when you are still a girl, to be wearing Playtex eighteen-hour underwires when the girls around you are wearing training bras, is to be a true alien. The big-breasted girl looks like a girl in a pornographic movie, "eye candy" in a school of boys who are just discovering their dad's basement stash of magazines. The boys look at her as if she is some sort of demented actress. The girls look at her as if she is an interloper, as if the extra amount of space she takes up is space she is stealing from them. The self-consciousness such attention can cause fostered an alienation so pronounced and deep among the girls I interviewed that I found myself understanding Madeline when she described this strange logic: she *suffered* for her breasts. "My girlfriends have had boob jobs, girls I see out in the clubs. And to me this isn't fair. These girls have these huge breasts overnight and I suffered, I suffered for years. They don't deserve those breasts."

Breasts and their associations of fertility become warped in the rumor mill; for the kids making quick, panicky associations, fertility is equated with the sex act, and so the girls whose bodies look like the bodies of mothers, of grown women, are assumed to be doing the things women do. Because their bodies have moved from childhood to adulthood so fast, these girls are assumed to be fast girls. The quickness of the body is extrapolated into a general quickness, a belief that she will go to bed with anyone in no time. The assumption is that the acts of the body create the body. "Big boobs meant you were having sex, I guess," says Margaret. Although she's still a virgin at twenty-six, Margaret's larger-than-life breasts made the kids think she'd been screwing around for years when she was only fourteen.

So the flesh and the shapes it takes are held as evidence of a girl's bad acts. This kind of logic prevails in the slut story: kids feel certain just by looking at her that they *know* what she's up to; they can just *tell.* Faced with this unflinching and irrational certainty, a girl might begin to wonder if the kids are right, if they know something she herself does not know. Listen to the rumors long enough and you will start to believe they are a sign of something. You will start to believe they're basically true.

3

THE SLUT ARCHETYPE

It is always difficult to describe a myth;
it cannot be grasped or encompassed;
it haunts the human consciousness
without ever appearing before it in
fixed form.

—Simone de Beauvoir, *The Second Sex*

Listening to these girls' voices, transcribing tapes in a cold office, I was presented again and again with variations of the same figure. After hearing a dozen girls tell essentially the same story, I realized that at the heart of these specific and isolated testimonies, a kind of cultural recurring dream was at work. Girl by girl, an identical *type* gained ascendancy, a universal girl who's gone too far, who can't come back, who has sinned beyond the periphery of redemption.

The high school slut has all the characteristics of a Jungian archetype. Rooted in the collective unconscious, the slut is an idea the mind carries within it and grafts on to the world. She is a projection of ancient dreams. When slut rumors occur, when the story is told and the roles are assigned, the narrative is always a reenactment, an echo. For the kids who take part in spreading rumors, they believe in her unquestioningly, just as they believe their own dreams when they are inside them.

In the transcripts of my interviews, between the lines of these particular girls' autobiographies, I could see the outlines of this archetype—it shifted and changed, but it was always present in some form. The slut archetype overpowered the self like a dream or a migraine. The girl in the rumors, the girl people saw when they looked at the slut, was part of an unconscious order that existed beyond my interview subjects, beyond their own histories. Becoming the slut, these girls saw reality edged out by a myth that reached back into the past and belonged not only to high school but to what Jung would call humankind.

As Jung defined the term, an archetype is a category of the unconscious. We fall into these categories and their associated images involuntarily. We just start telling stories or dreaming dreams, with no idea where they're coming from or why we need them so desperately. Jung used the idea of archetypes to explain the way humankind returns and returns to the same mythic structures. In his blustery, poetic texts he created an unforgettable image of the mind held captive by timeless visions. Reading Jung, one is tempted to believe that nothing new has ever happened, that the world is made up of a few inescapable tales and we participate in them automatically, gripped by the hand of destiny, maybe the hand of God.

Jung was writing in the 1930s and 1940s, and although his texts attempt a tone of universal objectivity, of distance and authority, they're awash in a subjective and personal misogyny that sometimes makes his books unreadable to an educated modern audience. Jung's sexism has been well documented by feminist critics. Nevertheless, despite his virtual inability to consider the "woman question" with any kind of insight, Jung was a genius. And as with any true genius, once the basic lessons of his work are comprehended, it is hard to shake them. In considering the power of the slut myth, I continually returned to Jung and his notion of archetypes. Again and again it struck me that the slut lived outside of time as Jung's archetypes do, and if the slut were ever to cease to exist, it would take nothing less than a seismic shift in the imagination of the world, a shift felt all the way down in the deepest layers of the collective unconscious.

In *Archetypes and the Collective Unconscious,* Jung described archetypes as "universal images that have existed since the remotest times." These images can be tracked through history in "certain continuities or modulations of the same figure." Archetypes form and delineate the subconscious and manipulate the conscious mind. They are like messages from an underground world, subliminal yearnings. For Jung, every image in a dream is a manifestation or extension of the self; conversely, the self is always caught in a dream, and one is never in full possession of the self because inexplicable images unravel the self's edges, making self-possession unattainable.

At the Calhoun High pep assembly, when the kids whisper into one another's ear, passing the rumor down the bleachers, they're participating in a communal, shared process. They're trying to free themselves of their own singularity. The rumor is a form of verbal and even physical connection: the cupped hand on your ear during the whisper, the way people come close when passing it on. It's a bond that seems vital even if it is only transitory. When the command is uttered, "Pass it on," it's assumed the person receiving the command will cooperate—there is an implicit faith that the kid who hears it next will understand the significance of the rumor and understand why it should not be questioned or stopped. Taking part in these whispering campaigns, kids feel like they belong. They're swept along by the crowd, and the crowd moves them out of the isolation of the self.

The reassuring quality of slut rumors and of archetypes in general is that they're forms of thought that seem to come from beyond the self and eclipse it. You want to belong to the crowd because you want to be rescued—from loneliness, from the fear of the day when there will be no one there, no one to pass it on to, no one coming toward you with news you need to know.

Jung wrote about the ways religious tales of heaven and hell resemble one another from faith to faith across the world. He believed the idea of God moved across history, manifesting as different myths, threading the past together, making a pattern where there was none before. Like religious seekers, the kids in high school want to make sense of the chaos of reality. They tell tales that populations have been telling for centuries, that divide up the world into sinners and saints, the cursed and the blessed.

The characters in high school myths, like the various gods and goddesses of the past, are clearly defined and embody distinct human traits. The "jock," the "cheerleader," the "nerd"—all these types can be effortlessly evoked in high school conversations, and it is clear what each one means. I remember learning that an old friend had been part of prom court in high school. "Oh, you were part of prom court?" we all asked, suspicious, certain this had deep-seated implications about his character and his capacity for ingratiation in the power structures of the larger world.

The "prom court attendant" is part of a powerful category. What's interesting about the slut as a category is (1) the way she is both powerful and powerless and (2) the way she is essentially a category of one. She in many ways defies the clear-cut systems of meaning within the school's civilization; she blurs the boundaries; she is the girl everyone despises but also the girl everyone remembers.

To become the slut is not to be associated with a group or a tribe; rather, it is to be singled out. In this way the slut as a figure is truly mythic—in the sense that specific mythical gods and goddesses embody specific human destinies. Like a character in a myth, the slut is a representative, a vessel of meaning, a messenger from an underground world of sex. The slut is never diluted by the presence of a crowd. Even if they had a group of girlfriends, the girls I interviewed always felt they had it harder than the other females around them.

Slut rumors hinge on the fear of female sexuality and its mystery; they evoke fear of the woman with a hole at the center of her body that is infinite, the black hole of feminine space into which a man could disappear. By turning one girl into the slut among them, the kids try to reassure themselves that they are on the right side of fate: They are good while she is evil. They are safe while she is unsafe. They have the right kind of desire while she has the wrong kind. In the haziness of sexual awakening, she is a clearly recognizable, boldly drawn cartoon. Like a monster in a monster movie, the slut appears in naive narratives of sex at a pivotal point—just when kids might be wondering what "too much" sex might mean and what a girl who wants too much sex might look like.

What is so monstrous about a sex-crazed girl? This is perhaps the question at the heart of the whole slut story.

No one rumor illustrates the archetypal quality of the slut story better than the legendary *train job*. The train job story goes something like this: a girl goes to a party/bar/locker room and gives fifty/seventy/a thousand boys blow jobs, one after another. Usually the story contains images of her swallowing cum or being covered with it. Although variations on the train job story have her giving oral sex while being entered in every other possible orifice, the train job is primarily an epic of oral sex. The story is a staple of high school, the college fraternity, and mainstream straight pornography.

In my interviews, we usually began talking about the train job rumor when I introduced the phrase "the whole football team." I would say, "What about 'the whole football team' thing? Did you ever hear that one?" This phrase inevitably brought eye rolling or groans of recognition before I had even finished my sentence, a heavy sigh as if to say, *Oh yeah, please, don't even go there!* It might not have been the football team—it could have been the soccer team, a motorcycle gang, the diving champions of the school. The point of the story was simply that there had to be a swarm of men up against one girl.

The appeal and formula of the train job plot relies on one girl's fantastic obedience. She moves from one man to another willingly and indiscriminately; they line up and she provides service. She is totally dependable and predictable.

Virtually every girl I interviewed was at some point in her slut career an object of this rumor. While some of the girls describe having sex with two or three men at once, the train job's image of a team, a vast and undifferentiated group of men, seems to be the stuff of pure fantasy. As far as I can tell from my interviews, the girl who services the entire football team is about as real as the tooth fairy. "Has *anyone* ever sucked off the football team, in *real life?*" Madeline asks this question with a thrilling cynicism in her voice.

Nevertheless, the train job is a plot so inescapable and persistent that to wonder whether it has actually happened or not is almost beside the point. It's happening everywhere, all the time. For the girls I interviewed, the train job was the story that pushed a girl over the edge from simply being "promiscuous" to being the high school slut. This was the particular set of graphic images that made everyone believe she was evil, she was doomed. The train job legend could irreversibly transform a girl's life and turn the world as she had known it inside out.

*　　*　　*

Sixteen-year-old Darby was known as the Blow Job Queen of her high school in California. In a note Darby sent me on a crumpled yellow piece of legal pad paper she wrote:

More rumors (none true)

I set up a chair at a party and got on my knees in front of it. I was drunk, and told everyone that if each gave me a joint, I'd give them a blow job.

Variation:

Three guys sat down on a couch, I took off all my clothes, and went down on the line one by one.

I meet Darby in a coffee shop in Seattle. Darby and her mother have moved here from California, and at sixteen she already feels like she is running away from something. She has decided to opt out of high school and take classes for a GED at night. She hasn't told her mom about her rotten experiences in the town where she grew up, how the slut rumors escalated and made her feel "totally insane." She hasn't told her twenty-two-year-old boyfriend, either. She hasn't really told anyone, but now she's telling me. I ask her why she wants to tell me and she says, "Maybe it's like free therapy?"

Darby tells me that her California town was a "crappy flat town where you walk through parking lots to get home." She describes herself as a girl who knew about "punk rock before anyone in my town knew punk rock was cool." She wears inch-thick black eye shadow, cutoff jeans, and ripped black tights. She describes "wanna-be Hell's Angels" riding after her on their motorcycles, saying, "Come home with me," because they heard she gave blow jobs for cigarettes. She talks about the one close girlfriend she had when she was fourteen. They sat outside on the lawn listening to the radio, painting their nails so they looked "totally porno."

Darby tells me her theories about how the rumors started: "At one party I went into the bathroom with this guy and made out with him. The next thing I knew the rumor was I had done everyone in the house in the bathroom! I think it all started with my first real boyfriend, Andrew. I was thirteen and he was seventeen. He was in a punk band and they sang a song about the slutty girls who worked at McDonald's. But I was so stupid I never put it all together. When the rumors about me got really bad, for a long time I couldn't figure out who had started it, and then I realized it was him, it was my boyfriend. All the time he was saying he loved me he was telling people I did circle jerks, or I gave head for a tab of speed." At sixteen, Darby wonders why she never put it all together, why she didn't make the connection between the songs her boyfriend was singing and the rumors that were washing over her in the hallways.

As the Blow Job Queen of her high school, Darby was pulled off course by the tide of an archetype. No matter how many times she tried to tell people, "That is not how it was," or, "That never happened," she couldn't get through to them. They were too enthralled with the dream of what she might have done to pay any attention to her protestations. The experience made her so wary of high school itself that she won't enroll again, even though she has moved thousands of miles, to a city where no one knows her.

*　　*　　*

It would seem that perhaps the origin, or breeding ground, of the train job story is pornography geared toward straight male consumers. *Debbie Does Dallas, Deep Throat*—the serial blow job is a best-selling formula. It might be the scenario that keeps the industry in business. In 1999 actress Annabelle Chong, known in porn circles for giving "the world's biggest gang bang" (servicing over 640 men) was interviewed by writer Jamie Hook in *The Stranger*, an alternative weekly. Hook is a film writer and the interview took place on the eve of the release of a documentary entitled *The Annabelle Chong Story*.

About the train job/gang bang scenario, Chong said: "The event is so much about male bonding, I think my presence is only supposed to guarantee the heterosexuality of the event. Really, most of the interaction that's going on is between the men. So it's a very homoerotic event. At some point the guys are standing in line; they're cruising each other, you know, checking each other out, kind of like, 'Hey, he's hard; I'm not; I better get hard soon—whoa, look at him! Isn't he big.' That sort of thing. So it becomes really competitive between the men, and there's a certain degree of backslapping going on."

Later Chong compares the train job scenario to sports, seeing both events as forms of homoeroticism disguised as contests of manliness.

While the train job fantasy centers around the willing, waiting girl, the story has nothing to do with the girl herself. The question of her pleasure is not asked; her appetites are obliterated. It's an especially comforting and safe fantasy because it eliminates the male's fear of personal inadequacy in the eyes of the female sex partner. Since there are so many men, there is nothing personal about it, and he cannot look her in the eyes for very long before another guy comes along. It also absorbs and absolves the male's fear of being perceived as a fag; men can stand next to one another in a fever of lust, side by side in the grip of it, but because the girl is there it means everything is all right. Everything is straight.

When Chong talks about the train job story, she refers to herself almost as if she's an extra—there to "guarantee the heterosexuality of the event" and to make sure that the boys have somewhere to release themselves. There is no room for a real girl in the plot; instead, the plot centers on an impossible girl whose mouth never tires, who can consume limitless amounts of cum without gagging, who *wants* this. In my interviews the question came up again and again—is there any girl who would want this?

Has the train job been invented by the straight pornography industry, or was the pornography industry invented because consumers needed to look at train job images? How does the chain of supply and demand work in this case? Whichever came first—the fantasy of the train job or the industry that promotes it—the scenario is continually being reasserted and reimagined. The woman who can take an infinite number of men inside her is continually re-created. Like a fairy tale, the train job legend has been recounted so many times it has become embedded in the fabric of the world.

*   *   *

One morning I type the word "slut" into the search engine of my computer. Over nine thousand sites come up, mostly porn, with an occasional stealthy feminist site slipping in. I click from one to another—Teenage Sluts, Slutty Catholic Schoolgirls. I examine blurred images of blow jobs, read the texts of various absurd plots in which the sex-starved nympho is lying in wait, just hoping to be overtaken. I look closely at my computer screen to see if I can detect any sadness in the eyes of the actresses. Usually I can't. I feel worked up. I feel as if I'm going to get in trouble, as if someone is going to open the door to my room and catch me in the act.

Until recently, American girls and women generally have not had much access to pornography. Women are the objects of pornography, but they have not been the subjects, the target audience. As a girl I remember another girl bringing a *Playgirl* to school once, but this was the extent of my exposure to images of nudity, much less graphic sex. In the early eighties beginning with the San Francisco scene, female-oriented sex shops started opening up around the country—still, as of this writing there are less than a dozen shops nationwide that sell videos, books, and sex toys primarily to a female clientele. The idea of women as unrestrained sexual consumers is relatively new and still on the margins.

For boys, pornography is a rite of passage, an accepted part of their becoming men. From the proverbial stories of discovering Dad's stash of magazines to the cliché of the high school boy with a *Playboy* hidden under his mattress, the discovery of pornography, like the discovery of masturbation, is considered part of boys' normal development. Masturbation is the way they release stress and pressure. Boys who do not masturbate are considered abnormal.

Girls do not have this culture of masturbation, nor do they have this graphic realm of sexual thought and speech; rather they have hints, romance tips, and teen idols. A graphic discussion of sex has no real place in adolescent feminine development. For girls the introduction into sex by and large lacks many visual elements at all, and the idea of physical climax as a way of releasing pressure is not widely discussed.

Because women have for so long been denied unmitigated access to the world of pornography, it's possible to see the Internet as a kind of frontier. Although there has been much lament about the evils of Internet pornography, the fact is that never before have women so effortlessly been able to observe and access the pornographic imagination of the culture. All it takes is a Web browser, and you are suddenly in the midst of it, the interior, viewing a realm of male dream life previously shut off behind closed doors, the intimidating doors of the topless club or porn theater. Sitting in my office surfing the Net, I feel a reflexive fear of getting caught, but really what I'm doing takes no risk and no initiative; it requires only turning on the computer, starting the search. This is a far cry from the idea of walking into a hard-core porn shop and thumbing through the selections along with the men.

Browsing the Web sites, I feel like I am looking through a keyhole into an adult world that in pre-Internet America had been mostly the province of adult males (except, of course, for the sex trade workers who keep it running). I can watch for as long as I want, and I will not have to wonder if anyone's watching me watching. I'm alone with the images, so I don't have to explain myself.

Most Internet porn sites, I soon discover, have installed a program or a set of commands that create a remarkable kind of technological sabotage. Whenever I try to click out of a site, or move back to my browser, I'm led further and further inside the site. I try to close the window on Slutty Catholic Schoolgirls, but the screen's immediately flooded by 12-Year-Old Hotties. *Are you sure you want to go?* the screen seems to ask. *Are you sure you have seen enough?* Later a computer expert tells me how this works: it's a piece of Java script that the porn sites have installed. What the script commands is this: the window should continuously replenish itself. Like casinos that are constructed to keep daylight out, many porn sites are constructed to keep people inside, so they will forget how much money they're spending and how long they've been gone.

These continually reappearing windows brought to mind the endless quality of the high school slut rumor, the way the girls who are on the inside of it cannot find a way to shut the story down. Every time a girl attempted to put an end to it, to shut down a sex rumor centered on her, a new and further distortion of the rumor would immediately spring to life. Like Jung's archetypes, the windows of the slut sites would not be suppressed. And no matter what commands or defenses a girl offered, the wild images of endless sex always came back to haunt her. They rose up again, as if by magic, just like they did on my computer screen.

*   *   *

When a girl is caught inside an archetype, she's aware of a separation between what people believe about her and what she believes about herself. No girl I interviewed said, *They were right, I did exactly what they said I did.* There was always a dissonance—a gap between the narrative of the crowd and the girl's own narrative. Because I was interested in the impact of rumors more than the consequences of actions, I didn't check out these women's pasts. When I'd interview a girl, I wanted to know what the kids said about her and how the rumors played out in her mind. I was far more interested in the narratives surrounding her than in figuring out whether or not she deserved her reputation.

Regardless of their actual sexual histories, many girls I interviewed talked about the moment when they started "acting slutty" after realizing that no matter what they said, the kids were going to believe the rumors anyway. Girls figured that since the reputation was so much bigger than they were, since it seemed to cast such a wide net, they might as well find a way to live within it and try to take possession of their identities after the fact.

Margaret dressed the part, shocking boys and girls alike with her low-cut T-shirts. "I said to myself, Well, now that they all think I'm this big whore, I might as well have some fun." Lucy went after guys at parties, sometimes kissing three in a night. "I wanted to be important," she wrote me in an e-mail, "and I knew how to achieve that, if only for a few hours." Erin talked about how being a slut made her feel like a somebody, and how she'd play it up when she was around other girls, relishing her power over them.

This sense that people know who you are, that the other kids remember your name effortlessly, maybe even dream of you, constitutes one of the intermittent pleasures of the slut experience. For many of the girls I interviewed, infamy brought with it a sense of being chosen, of mattering. They knew one thing: they weren't invisible. When they walked in the door, everyone knew they were there. Everyone had been waiting for them to arrive.

Of course, there's a vast underside to being notorious. Even if the girls I interviewed sometimes felt like shining beings or celebrities, they also lacked much sense of control over their lives. When they became the school slut, they lost their sense of privacy; they felt their true selves had been erased by the girl people said they were. The slut gossip, stirring some collective need of both boys and girls, became stronger and more resilient than the girl herself. Suzanne, a twenty-one-year-old from Philadelphia, wrote in her e-mail, "Whenever you would fight it, they assumed you were covering it up." Madeline, the Calhoun High refugee, talked about how she didn't do "half of the things they said about me." Everyone said she cheated on her boyfriend but she never had, although she does admit to flirting and generally behaving like a disobedient, troubled girl. "I was a wild child," she says. Maybe kids were trying to tame her with their rumors and nicknames. After a couple of years of slut rumors, Madeline started to feel like the other kids had invented her. Pointing to herself, she says, *"This* is what they created." Madeline gives up her own agency. She says, in essence: This is beyond me. *They* did this.

Madeline's sense that she is being constructed and reconstituted by the kids surrounding her proves common among the girls I interview. I begin to interpret this me-versus-them attitude as an expression of powerlessness under the weight of an archetype. Like Jung's secret life that seems to hold sway in the unconscious, girls who are labeled the high school slut perceive their lives to be determined by the beliefs and needs of the crowd's dirty mind. They are captives of the collective unconscious. They did not ask to be in the middle of this story, but here they are, regardless.

In a horror movie marketed to teens in the summer of 1999, *Disturbing Behavior,* the oversexed girl meets a predictably violent end. The plot of *Disturbing Behavior* hinges on the idea that the entire high school football team has been taken over by aliens. In the opening scene, the camera pans onto a car parked above a reservoir. A boy and girl make out in the front seat, the girl straddling the boy, kissing him anxiously. The boy holds back as windows fill with steam. After repeatedly pushing her away, the boy explains to the girl that he needs to preserve his "vital fluids" for the big game tomorrow. The girl looks at him mischievously, then unzips his pants; her head disappears into his lap. The boy's eyes flash red (the first clue to his alien status) and he breaks her neck with his hands. "Slut," he mutters in the direction of the lifeless girl.

Disturbing Behavior was one in a long line of horror films marketed toward teenagers in the late nineties, a period in which this perennial genre flourished. The most infamous and successful among these films were the *Scream* series, directed by Wes Craven. The *Scream* series was popular in part because it played on kids' sense of knowing and irony; it assumed that kids had seen so many horror movies that they knew the formulas by heart.

In horror movies, the murder of the slut is the first lesson in a series of lessons about what happens when you wander out into the sexual darkness. As the formula goes, the promiscuous girl is always the first to get killed in the bloodbath. The girl who asks for sex is going to *get it*—not just sex but also her own physical destruction. Her lust and her destruction are always intertwined.

For horror movie buffs the classic sex-leads-to-dead-girl scene is from *Friday the 13th,* where a fresh-faced camp counselor who has just finished having sex with her boyfriend stares at herself in the mirror, humming and admiring herself in her underwear. The ominous music begins as she grows lost in her own reflection—if only she could take her eyes off herself, she would see what's coming. The knife blade flashes and the girl is transported from bliss to terror in an instant.

Although the majority of kids viewing horror films have become very sophisticated in their understanding of pop culture and believe they know exactly what will happen next, what happens still causes a rush inside their skin. Like pornography, horror movies cause a visceral thrill, a physical surge of expectation. The plot of the destroyed promiscuous girl can be a cliché only because it is so inevitable. Like clockwork the girl is killed; the audience knows it will happen and there is no sense of shock or surprise. But this does not mean that the narrative's predictability has freed them of an essential belief in the narrative itself. Kids still treat certain girls among them as if they are and have always been bad, as if they're only getting what is coming to them. In the advancement of the slut archetype, in the narrative of the collective dream, the girl who *wants it* is always the one inviting her own violent end.

"I had this dream I was back in my hometown," Darby, from California, tells me. "And I was stabbed to pieces in front of a crowd of numb onlookers." Darby tells the dream to prove how deep her feeling of dread of the California slut period goes, all the way down into the tissues. She tells it slowly and purposefully, gesturing with her graceful black fingernails. "I was being killed, and no one did anything!"

Darby's dream of all the people watching her get destroyed is an essential dream at the base of the slut experience. Images of destruction are integral to the story of the slut, since she must be destroyed for everyone else to move toward the light; she must be sacrificed in the mythic progress toward enlightenment. This is her role, this is her place—to be touched and then destroyed.

When Odysseus sailed past the Sirens and was tempted, he made it past temptation, back toward the homeland of love. At the edge of the love story—where the love story ends and the confusing pornographic dream begins—the slut is positioned like the Siren singing. She needs to be reckoned with, but anyone with any integrity, any hero, will eventually sail past and leave her behind.

Her singing must be subdued and silenced; in modern horror movies, her heart must be stopped by an attacker as she sings into the mirror, full of herself, full of her own voice. Given the plethora of images of destruction surrounding slutty women, it's not surprising that the girls I interviewed absorbed these images and started to see themselves reflected in them. In a culture that annihilates oversexed women, girls who have been ordained the high school slut often want to destroy themselves.

Girls reported suicide attempts, stays in psych wards, a life on and off medication, in and out of addiction. When the specter of self-destructive tendencies entered my conversations with older women, I would sometimes ask, "Well, how are you feeling about your life now?" and invariably I would get an answer such as, "Not very good. I am barely holding on. I wanted to kill myself then, and often I want to kill myself now." I heard stories of wrists cut, pills swallowed and then stomachs pumped, a heroin overdose, a night spent driving ninety miles per hour without headlights.

What is the connection between the high school slut archetype and girls with suicidal tendencies? In a pamphlet passed out to high school counselors about suicide prevention in 1999, promiscuity is listed among a series of warning signs of suicide. Other items on the list include pot smoking, sudden changes in grades, and increased talk about death and dying. This particular pamphlet is not gender specific, but considering that boys, as one girl put it, "can be studs without anything bad happening to them," it's not a leap of logic to assume that the dangerously promiscuous teenager isn't a stud but a slut. Girls who move from boy to boy indiscriminately are tempting fate, flirting with death. They are exhibiting a desire to die.

Maybe self-destructive girls are the lightning rod for sex rumors, or maybe rumors catalyze the self-destructive impulse. I am not sure where the beginning is, but my interviews convinced me of a link, a thematic way one plays off the other. That my interviews supported the connection between high school sluts and suicidal tendencies doesn't prove, of course, that promiscuity *itself* is a warning side of suicide. But the slut drama and its rituals of negation, the way the girl is treated like a contaminated and worthless soul—these are experiences that can easily evoke a dormant desire to make oneself vanish, to retreat back into the darkness from which one originated.

One of the most depressed women I interviewed was Kate, a hairdresser in New Jersey. Kate grew up in a middle-class suburb, loved "the Boss," and partied at the Jersey shore with her friends, everyone passing whiskey bottles around, building fires out of sticks and trash. She attended a big public high school, where she was on the fast track toward good grades. But she had a style that hid her brainiac tendencies: smoking pot, teasing her hair and wearing tons of makeup, going to college parties, playing "Born to Run" full blast as she drove into the school parking lot.

Kate locates the beginning of the slut rumors with her first boyfriend, a skateboarding boy with a sweet face and a big mouth. "I was fifteen and this guy, I didn't know him well, he had just come to town. Visiting his mom or something. And we had sex together, really great. And he left. But the next fall he moved back to town, and he found out I'd had sex with two other guys since he'd left. And he said, 'I have created a monster.'"

Pretty soon this boy spread rumors about her. He wanted the other kids to believe she was a monster, too, so he went about creating her. He yammered on about how she would do anything, and before long everyone knew about it. According to Kate, she'd start dating someone, then he'd hear about her reputation and break up with her. "Guys would talk to each other about sex. And they'd say, 'Kate is really good at sex.' And then they'd say, 'You know why Kate knows what to do? 'Cuz she's a slut.'"

Kate is proud of her sexual abilities and during our interviews refers repeatedly to the way she drives men crazy by knowing "what to do." Yet this pose of confidence is inevitably undercut by a palpable self-loathing. She describes her past as "a cesspool" and talks about how she frequently dreams of suicide.

Kate ends up telling me the story of a night under the Jersey boardwalk when she got what the proverbial slut is "asking for," when the fantasies of pornography coincided with the formulas of horror.

"Me and my girlfriends got these guys to buy us beer and we went down to the beach. I went under the boardwalk with this one guy. I had sex with him willingly because he reminded me of my ex-boyfriend. He turned out to be nothing like him, he just looked like him.

"After we were done he took my pants and my underwear and hid them. Then he came back with four other guys, and they all surrounded me. I felt really scared and vulnerable. I had no pants. I didn't know where I was gonna go. They were all together but they only did things one at a time. But there was always someone else there, I was never alone with just one guy.

"I remember the word 'pig' came out, that I wanted it and what a pig I was. Then it went on, and I know I blocked out more terrible things because it was so painful. And they kept my underwear as a souvenir. I had a feeling from their conversation that they had done this to other girls, too. They were freako rejects under the boardwalk. They were older. What saved me from being really angry at them was they were such losers. The guys at school who treated me like a slut, I am more angry with them because at least they probably came from decent homes.

"I got worse after the boardwalk thing in a way. It was like, oh well, it doesn't matter anymore. And I had a suicide attempt. This was definitely something that took me years to get out. I turned it onto myself. Even though part of me was like, no, it wasn't my fault, this isn't what I wanted at all. But then there was a part of me that was like, well, you were there, and were you hurt? No. Did they beat you up? No. Did I try hard enough to fight it? Maybe not."

Kate talks about what happened to her that night with a mixture of rage and resignation. She presents this crime as a piece of twisted logic, as the most inevitable horror story outcome of her slut narrative. She's angry with these men, but she never pressed charges. She thinks of that dark night as something that had been coming her way all along. When she talks about the men, she says it seemed to her they had done this before. They seemed accustomed to the whole scenario. As Kate renders it, the men beneath the boardwalk were acting out an assigned role.

The more Kate tried to bury the memory of that night, the more suicide loomed in the back of her mind. Everywhere she looked, she saw clues to the buried story. The scene beneath the boardwalk was like those windows on my computer that refused to close; it stayed there, even when she tried every way she knew to turn it off.

When Carl Jung assigned his archetypes to the world, positing the notion that people cannot free themselves of certain stories, he was both describing the West's thematic obsessions and reestablishing deeply rooted patriarchal hegemonies. If his texts move forward on currents of poetry, they also carry a backward current: they rely on a profound malevolence toward women. In *Aspects of the Feminine* he writes about the archetype of female "animus," which in many ways resembles the slut archetype I've been discussing here: the female who is insatiable and illusory, full of irrational and colossal desires. Jung writes, "No matter how friendly and obliging a woman's Eros may be, no logic on earth can shake her if she is ridden by the animus. Often the man has the feeling—and he is not altogether wrong—that only a seduction or a beating or a rape would have the necessary power of persuasion."

The slut story and the train job, the promiscuous girl

meeting a terrible end—these stories are part of the cultural weather for kids on both sides of them. Whether kids are spreading the rumors or enduring their consequences, these stories sway, bend, and delineate the imagination. They are a fantastically hostile inheritance.

4

THE DANGEROUS SUBURB

Subdivisions with reassuring names, cul-de-sacs, families driving around in four-door cars; outposts of chain restaurants and extremely green lawns and mostly white people. Suburban Stepford Wives America was the setting for the stories of many girls I interviewed, the backdrop against which the slut drama was enacted. Often, even before the girls evoked it directly, I could detect this America in their voices, their accents, their slang. Girls from white suburbia proved my most adamant and effortless interview subjects. Demographically, they were girls for whom the word itself—"slut"—had an undeniable charge that inspired them to talk. And through the act of talking, through the bridge of a conversation, they hoped to deplete the word of some of its impact.

Why does the slut story seem to flourish in the suburban landscape? Maybe the answer can be located in Shibutani's generalizations about populations susceptible to rumor: that often an atmosphere of monotony becomes a breeding ground for exaggerated storytelling. The slut rumor is a way of bringing a hint of scandal and recklessness to a place of uniform, serene surfaces and perfectly timed traffic lights. It is an attempt to interrupt and undermine this world, maybe glamorize it. One girl remembers spreading rumors about a slut in her small suburban town: "It was so exciting to talk about her. She was mythic. We would walk by her house every day going home from school and hope to see her in the window." Additionally, suburban high schools often cultivate a thriving jock culture and therefore rumors like the whole-football-team story can effortlessly spread and take on formidable velocity and currency in a short amount of time.

"In the burbs everyone thinks they're safe," says twenty-three-year-old Louise. She attended a school of all white kids in the midst of a cluster of subdivisions; to her, these kids seemed far more invested in the slut story than anyone she met when she finally moved to Manhattan. Of course, Louise's generalization about "everyone" does not apply to real people, but it is an idea deeply embedded in the dream of suburbia: that it is a place somehow safe from the hordes. In this seemingly safe place, the girl rumored to move outside the safety zone becomes the center of attention, the object on which kids focus their gaze as they search for visual stimulation. "Look, look," the kids say, hungry for sights; "there she is." And the geography of suburbia guarantees that rumors about her will spread—a story recounted on a bathroom wall in one building will be written in a note passed in class in another building down the street. The buildings are almost identical, the structures echo one another, and so the girl can be easily translated. In the ordered landscape, the disorderly girl quickly becomes infamous.

Thirty-five-year-old Karen Lehman is one of these suburban refugees; after a couple of phone interviews she agrees to take me on a tour of the landscape of her past. We meet on a Saturday in the lobby of the downtown Pittsburgh Marriott hotel. Earlier on the phone, when I asked her what she looks like, she said, "I'm fat. No one would guess that I was the huge whore of my high school." At the Marriott, I walk around the brass-and-pink-marble fountain a few times, surveying the room. There's piped-in music and the thick smell of air freshener. Outside, the Pittsburgh afternoon looks so gray it's as if there has been an eclipse.

I locate Karen sitting on one of the plush couches by the check-in desk, reading *USA Today*. She's a pretty, olive-skinned woman who's letting her hair grow out after years of dye jobs. She slouches in her clothes, uneasy in her body. We take the elevator underground to where she has parked her car—a ten-year-old gray Honda with crystals hanging from the rearview mirror. "This car is my baby," she says. "It has totally saved my life because when things get really bad, I can just get inside and drive."

The place we're headed toward is called Andover Heights, the suburban ground zero of Karen's slut period.

She hasn't been back for a few years, ever since she moved away from the "high school hellhole" in her early thirties. She talks about moving away from Andover Heights as a form of rescuing herself; she had been suffering from major depression, and once admitted herself to a psychiatric facility. She tells me this as I notice a pile of addiction and recovery pamphlets on the car floor. Now she lives in New Jersey in an apartment complex with a courtyard pool. People live there whom Karen recognizes as "bad influences"—a band of druggies always hanging out poolside—and she tries to avoid them. But she is a woman with a powerful self-destructive streak, and she doesn't trust herself completely. She hopes she has finally freed herself, but she can't be sure.

Karen laughs easily and listens intently, but waves of mistrust come over her suddenly like strokes. All at once her eyes blacken with anger. "Could you take your sunglasses off?" she asks. "I need to look people in the eye when I talk to them." At certain points during our visit I'll feel a little afraid of her, of how deep she might go into the dark region of her memory, where the secrets are so difficult they threaten to unravel her fragile self-possession. "I don't know how long I can talk to you," she says, "before my mind closes the door on all this."

We reach Andover Heights, a hamlet of quaint brick buildings, old-fashioned "shoppe" signs, immaculate and identical houses. Once we reach the city center Karen's demeanor changes. She seems genuinely spooked. She drives like she's forgetting how to drive. At a stoplight she locks eyes with a man crossing the street; he stares through the windshield, a pale, hunched bundle of nerves sporting Coke-bottle glasses.

When the light changes and we escape his gaze Karen says, "You know what is so freaky? *He* could be one of the guys who spread all those rumors about me, and I wouldn't know. I look around here and I'm wondering: Were you one of them? Were you? Is that why you are looking at me like that?" Her paranoia is contagious; throughout our visit I will watch people watching her, and wonder if they're part of the mob from the past.

Karen's bad reputation started on her first day of junior high at a private Catholic school and followed her throughout adolescence. "Seventh, eighth, ninth, and tenth grades were the worst. I started going to these parties, and they were, like, spin-the-bottle parties. Everybody was doing it. You play spin the bottle, kiss boys. I did it too and I thought I was with them, but after a while it was like the girls didn't want to talk to me anymore.

"I learned my phone number was written on all these places around school. Oh my God, it was horrible. It was like all of a sudden—we're talking about seventh grade in a Catholic school, and the kids wouldn't talk to me. I was branded. Everywhere I went they called me a whore. You know it was like I was Mary Magdalene. It never stopped. Wherever I went, the girls either wouldn't talk to me or they wanted to beat me up. I got mercilessly beat up by girls. I always had girls I didn't know calling me up and yelling, 'I heard you wanna go out with my boyfriend!' And I had no idea who these girls were. The boys were no better. They'd throw rocks at me. Literally, they would throw rocks at me when I was walking home from school."

She shows me the school yard where kids yelled "Whore"

at her, where a boy stole her book bag and wrote H-O-R-E on it in permanent marker. She points out the statue of the Virgin guarded by a KEEP OFF THE GRASS sign on which someone once wrote, FOR A GOOD TIME CALL KAREN. Nearby there's the patch of grass where a couple of heavy metal girls jumped her and beat her up, threatening to cut off her long hair. And there is the shaded doorway where she once took a stand, throwing down her guitar case and yelling, "*What the fuck* is up with you girls, anyway!" We sit down in the shade and she points to a white wall bordering the playground. "I kissed a boy behind there once, a kiss I totally remember." Even now, the kiss lives separately from everything else, a small shimmer of romance, a lip lock that can still make her shiver with delight.

If boys offered escape it was always momentary; sooner or later they would turn on her, call her Two Dollars because they heard that's how much she charged for blow jobs. The nicknames attached themselves to Karen and stayed with her; she no longer had any control over her name or her story. She was held captive by the other kids' dirty minds and by the stories of sin on which they thrived. Sooner or later the lies would inevitably make their way back to her: she did it with a bunch of guys behind a tombstone in the cemetery; they all lined up and she let them.

Girls came forward as eyewitnesses: *Yeah, we saw her there, it's a fact.* These girls were considered reliable witnesses: they were popular, they had Dorothy Hamill haircuts, and they had known from day one that Karen was sick or evil. Maybe they knew someone who knew someone who had seen her giving a blow job in the middle of a well-lit room, or they'd heard from their boyfriends about a train job that went on and on into infinity. Boys corroborated the stories, claiming they had "done" her. "All the boys said they had fucked me or I had sucked their dicks," says Karen, "and I had never done anything with any of them."

Karen was born in the American dust bowl but she did not live there very long—one of the Dakotas, a place that is nothing to her except some prairie shadows. When she was three years old, her family moved to South Philly, which she considers her spiritual home.

"It was this really small, close-knit Italian community. The church bells would ring a couple of times a day. None of the kids swore. It was this amazingly pure place. None of the kids stole, or talked about sex." Karen idealizes South Philly in our conversation; she wants me to see that things were not always so dark for her. She wants to render an interval of light. So although South Philly is one of the most crime-ridden areas in the country, Karen's descriptions of her life there are positively Edenic: the love of the family flowing like a river, her mother and real dad and brother home every night for dinner. She remembers believing in ideas like "All good things come to those who wait" and the afterlife. "You know, it was this beautiful childhood," she says. "This beautiful, pure childhood. The nuns teaching these great little lessons about heaven and stuff."

But then the light falls out of the story bit by bit. Karen's mother divorces when she's still in elementary school. The parents who together had created you kissing across the dinner table—this version of destiny was not to be. Her mom would pace around crying, often forgetting to pick Karen up from school or lessons. Karen would wander around the neighborhood talking to anyone, including strangers and street people. She still loved South Philly, but she started to feel most at home out on the street, where she could find distractions from her loneliness. She no longer wanted to be inside the house, where all she could do was wait around and be reminded of sad things.

A time came when her mother thought she found what she'd been waiting for: a stepdad came heroically through the front door, vowing to rescue her and her children with love and money. Within a very short period, however, Dad number two wore out, grew mean, went broke, left the picture. Karen, who was ten years old at the time, remembers a lot of slamming doors, her mother crying desperately, "getting the crap beat out of her." By the time Dad number three arrived, Karen was twelve years old, but she felt much older. She felt like she had been on earth too long already.

Dad number three worked an office job with opportunities for advancement, and when he was awarded a good promotion, he decided that the family would move to Andover Heights. Everyone seemed overjoyed. Karen tried to feign happiness about moving to this foreign Andover Heights country where families had big yards and top-of-the-line appliances, where grown men and women reflexively attached balloons to mailboxes whenever there were birthday parties or babies born, and where kids had trampolines and could often be seen rising and falling over the horizon of their houses, as if trying to build the momentum to fly out of there for good.

But after a short amount of time in Andover Heights,

Karen began to wonder if her mother was all there. She seemed too gung ho about the dream of this clean place where she could start over, erase the memory of the previous husbands. Karen's mother wanted so much from suburbia; she wanted it to be a place where no one has ever been beaten, where no one has been disappointed, where you get what you deserve, not what is coming to you.

When Karen talks about her mother's wishfulness, it seems she's getting at the root of why she hates this place so much—she believes it is hiding something, that it is pretending to be safe when it isn't. She resents the landscape as virulently as she resents the kids who lived within it and the dads who abandoned her family within it. Despite the promises of safety, Andover Heights seemed far more dangerous to Karen than the deepest inner city could ever be. It was a promised land that broke all its promises, a finite migration into the middle class that exacted an infinite price.

The notion that suburbia might be hiding something is, of course, not a new idea. It's a notion used to create suspense in horror films or TV movies. In the movie of the week cliché the sun shines too brightly on white fences and the viewer knows something violent is about to happen. For the girls I interviewed, this stock method of rendering suburbia was often another way of describing their pervading sense of a split between myth and reality. In this way the whole idea of the suburb where *things are not what they seem* was a metaphor. Further, it was a way of talking about issues of class, which are integral to the slut experience—as I discussed earlier, many girls did not feel like they were classy after being branded the slut, and they wondered if they would ever feel like they had any value. "We moved to a good neighborhood," one girl told me, "and the new school was full of rich bitches who called me a slut and wrote *White Trash* on our mailbox."

These girls were suspicious of the suburban dream of crossing over into a better class in part because their own experience had made them suspicious of the very notion of upward mobility. They felt so paralyzed by the dirty mind of the crowd, movement itself seemed impossible. Attempts were made to escape the net of rumors, to find a passage out: another group of friends, a counselor who might reason with the whispering kids, another school altogether. Yet no matter how much agency and ambition these girls displayed, hoping to pull themselves up out of the sexual ghetto, more often than not they always ended up back in the midst of the rumors.

In the annals of books about sex and suburbia, one title is often cited: *Our Guys: The Glen Ridge Rape and the Secret Life of the Perfect Suburb* by Bernard Lefkowitz. A sensational volume that went on to become a TV movie, Lefkowitz's book is a detailed and exhaustive piece of reporting on the gang rape of a mentally slow girl by "our finest boys"—captains of the football team, jock heroes in a school that valued athletics above all other endeavors. As Lefkowitz renders it, the jock-worshiping culture of the high school caused the boys to get drunk on power. They started to believe they could get away with anything and that they were beyond recrimination or punishment. One day they lured a girl, known in town as retarded, into a basement, repeatedly raped and sodomized her, and then embarked on a campaign of silence.

The suspense of *Our Guys* requires that readers believe in the suburban cliché of safety. Lefkowitz plays on and exploits this belief in his retelling of the rape of Glen Ridge. The guys in the title are presented as the kind of guys we would never expect to be capable of sexual violence. These are guys with girlfriends, glory, the world spread out before them. The reader is shocked to learn that "our guys" might not be who we thought they were, that even in a perfect place and in the midst of a perfect life, our dear sons will lead girls down into basements and move across moral boundaries toward a nihilism usually associated with unsafe urban areas.

Since Lefkowitz's book concerned a sex crime, jacket copy trumpeted it as a study revealing "the hidden world of unrestrained adolescent sexuality." Besides relying on stereotypes of the suburbs, the narrative also relied on a subtler insinuation, that there are girls these things "happen to" and then there are girls whom these things should never happen to.

Lefkowitz divides the girls of Glen Ridge into categories: (1) the girls who went out with "our guys"—girlfriends and cheerleaders, (2) the girl who is the victim at the center of the story, who stands alone, and (3) the girls who are sluts. In a revealing passage, Lefkowitz writes: "Everyone was saying the same thing, the victim was a slut." Yet Lefkowitz argues, she was *not* a slut, because her mental disability made her helpless. She did not know what she was doing. Implicit in his argument is the notion that if she had been a slut, we might not be so shocked at what happened to her; we might even understand it.

In an attempt to find the story of girls who voluntarily commit the kinds of acts that occurred in the basement, Lefkowitz interviews a clique called the "little mothers." Like the Dorothy Hamill look-alikes in Karen's courtyard, the little mothers are judges in the realm of sex. They're called little mothers because they seem like the kind of girls who will grow up and get married. They have lots of friends, they're friendly with the jocks, and they exhibit all the symptoms of girls headed for a good, normal future.

As Lefkowitz makes clear, the little mothers were the girls who did not have sex with the jocks but were friends with them, girls who saw all the sexual outrageousness but did not take part in it. They were witnesses to the aforementioned "unrestrained world of adolescent sexuality." According to one of the little mothers, "A girl who gave blow jobs to guys one after another was nicknamed 'Seal.' . . . The girl was behaving 'like a trained seal in the circus, doing whatever they commanded.'" Another girl, called Angie, appears in a section called "All American Guys": "Angie would remember nights when one of the Jocks would go upstairs with one of the girls and come down a little while later and declare loudly to his buddies, 'I just got a blow job from her.' Then he'd cock his head toward the stairs, as if to say, You're next in line if you want it. Another link in the chain of fraternal bonding."

Lefkowitz buys Angie's story and passes it on as readily as a kid in an assembly. He never imagines his way up the stairs, behind the closed door. He never hears the "seal" girl's version of events. He assumes that what the little mothers said happened actually happened. He assumes the slut must always exist somewhere in the heart of the suburb, doing what sluts do, obediently giving train jobs to lines of hungry boys.

For the retarded girl who did not "ask for it," the boys in the basement are criminals, but what about the girls at the party who did ask for it, or who everyone claims asked for it and got it? Where do they fit in the story? When Lefkowitz recounts the stories of parties, passed down from the little mothers, he creates a narrative equivalency between the sexual acts that "happened" at those parties and the rape that victimized the retarded girl. Because the boys had reportedly done things like this before, they were expecting to do it again. Thus the slut girls are inadvertently responsible: they have created an expectation of a vast opening where you can do anything and put anything. It is the slut who corrupts our guys.

If Lefkowitz posed the question "How could such bad things happen in the American suburb?" as a suburban refugee Karen wondered just the opposite: "How could *this* *not* happen here?" For Karen, the landscape of Andover Heights itself, this unnatural manifestation of white flight, created the conditions where kids acted uncivilized and called her terrible names, chasing after her in the school yard like they wanted to annihilate her. Maybe, she thinks, she should have known, she should have seen it coming. She says, "I mean, *look around,* look at this nightmare!"

A banner in an elementary school window reads: NEW KNOWLEDGE NEW FRIENDS A NEW YEAR. A road sign reads: DEAF CHILD IN AREA.

Karen says, "I never should have been here. I was the

kind of girl who liked to shock people by wearing weird socks, or refusing to brush my hair."

We pull up at the address where Karen first lived when her family moved to Andover Heights, a brick row house with a thin strip of front yard. This is the poor district, where people live so close together they know the exact sound of their neighbor's car or the tenor of their children's voices. Karen remembers a boy lived next door who was obsessed with the movie *Jaws* and only wore T-shirts advertising it. Across the street there's a house where Jim Croce once lived for a short time, a fact that has become part of the town's mythology. When Karen first arrived, she would look out her bedroom window and see the woods. Now that window looks out toward more houses, multiplying to the horizon.

Karen continues telling me her story as we drive away from her old neighborhood. She talks about how near the end of the era of Dad number three, after she'd been the school slut for five years, she started having elaborate fantasies: she once dreamt she was the May queen, elected by the school to place a crown of flowers on the Virgin at the end of the year. In the dream kids applauded and worshiped her. Many of her fantasies centered on memories of South Philly: its decrepit streets and apartments crowded together, the way people greeted her as if she mattered, acknowledging her as she passed by with barely perceptible nods that seemed to say, *You are fine, you are fine, don't worry*. She dreamed of moving back there and being a little girl again.

Because Karen has always been a sentimental person, trust found her even when she was sure it had gone into permanent hiding. One day in the cafeteria she trusted a girl who seemed nice and unthreatening, a good listener. Karen told the girl a secret from her past that was very important to her.

"I thought this girl was my friend, and so I started telling her about Baba. He was this man who lived there in the old neighborhood; he was kind of a mythic figure. He was really short, and he was like mentally retarded or something. He had this dent in his head. He was very weird looking. And we called him Baba because that was all he could say. I felt really sorry for him. Everybody knew him but no one knew what was wrong with him. He wore glasses, and he had these beautiful blue eyes. I remember one day as a little kid staring into his eyes for a long time.

"I was thinking of him there at the Catholic school in Andover Heights, and I was missing him. And I told this girl about him. This girl—I thought she was my friend—she used this story I told her to make up a lie about me. And by the time the rumor got back to me everyone said that in South Philly I lived with my retarded father, and I fucked him all the time. She told it so Baba was my father, and oh yeah, yeah, they said he was half sheep, and I let him fuck me."

The distortion of this story by the rumor mill is a remarkable example of the way anything about Karen could be completely transformed to serve the kids' own beliefs about her freakishness. After she found out about the blue-eyed-man rumor, Karen tried not to think about his pure eyes anymore, or the sun on the streets in South Philly, or the girl who seemed to listen to her that day at lunch. Baba had turned from myth into monster, transformed by talk, by whispers, by the sexually naive, hormonally crazed imaginations of kids who want to gross one another out. Walking home from school, Karen would wait for the kids to come out with their rocks. "Two Dollars! Two Dollars!" The rocks sailed through the air toward her, as if words had turned into real, solid things.

At times Karen wondered what she ever did to deserve this hell, if maybe God was trying to tell her something. She felt chosen and persecuted—the persecution was so relentless and graphic she felt almost famous. One day she etched her name into a metal lid, then buried it in the front walkway flower beds. So many people had written her name in so many places: phone booths, locker rooms, the sign in front of the Virgin. Maybe if she wrote it here, herself, on this stupid metal lid, she would take possession of her name again.

5

FAMILY VALUES AND HOME WRECKERS

Where does the archetype begin? How far back does it go? I know that when I trace back through my own memory, the idea of the slut and the idea of a woman who might be destroyed by sex were present from an early age, at early moments of self-consciousness and exploration of the feminine.

When we were kids, my mother warned me and my two sisters about what happened to girls who had too much sex. "You get shopworn!" she said. In the bedroom of my grandmother's house, where we visited many weeknights at cocktail hour, the three of us tried on lipstick and chiffon scarves that reeked of mothballs. We would sashay in front of the mirror and say, "Hello, darling. Hello, darling," batting our eyelashes.

We knew there was something whorish about what we were doing, something transgressive about the flirtatious tone in our voices and the way we would say, "Darling, darling," to invisible boyfriends. Was this the way girls who were shopworn acted? We were putting on a freak show of femininity.

Downstairs, the adults were absorbed by their cocktails, and they usually forgot about us. If we were gone too long, or if our laughter took on the edge of dirty talk, an adult might yell up the staircase, "What's going on up there?" At the sound of the voice, we'd run into the bathroom, wash the lipstick off our faces, and go back down to the kitchen. My grandfather came up the driveway around six, and we were there with the extended family to greet him. Settled into the kitchen, he sat quietly eating cheese and crackers, with his suit still on, his tie loosened, the bourbon beginning to relieve him sip by sip. "Pretty girls, pretty girls," he would say, and we'd flutter around him like angels, like the perfect girls we wanted him to believe in.

My sisters and I washed our faces to hide the truth of the game we had been playing in the bedroom. We instinctively had a sense of how girls were and were not supposed to act and we knew in some way that trouble would come if we emerged and showed ourselves in the lipstick and seductive charade that gave us such a rush of pleasure. This game was like a thrilling secret threading us together as we sat there acting good.

Browsing the shelves of the University of Washington library in the sex section, I come across a small paperback document called *Man's Unconscious Passion*, published in 1920. It's a short, two-hundred-page pamphlet bound between hard plastic covers to keep it from falling apart, and it hasn't been checked out for many years. The author, Wilfred Lay, writes in a convoluted prose style that is often hard to decipher, but the gist of his argument is that men need to learn to direct their unconscious lustful impulses toward the right kind of woman, otherwise they will inhabit unreal relationships and fragmented lives. It's like a training manual about temptation: how to see it coming, how to be calm and reasonable in the face of it. Lay describes the attraction toward a loose woman as an attraction that causes a forgetting of the family and a forgetting of society itself: "If a man were able to transfer his affection to a woman outside of the pale of social respectability, he would have to dispose of all his ideas consciously acquired from contact with his family—ideas which, in his fore-conscious, have been integrated into a code of morality containing modes of emotional reaction antipathetic to women of loose morals." Later he considers the role of the female in the melodrama of sexual corruption: "No woman with perfect love united of affection . . . and insight, can potentially approach the condition of looseness. Her feelings are all attached to the same man, and the right man, and her devotion is complete and final."

The world that Lay envisions here is a world of opposites, in which the loose woman is the opposite of the "intact" woman, and the man who feels affection for her is moving in the opposite direction of family life. The intact woman either is literally a virgin or, even after she has been deflowered, thinks about sex only in the right way, her thoughts all moving upward, toward heaven—her thoughts are intact even if her hymen isn't. She has never swayed from monogamy and, as Lay so memorably phrases it, she is always attached to "the same man, and the right man."

In 1930 Catholic philosopher Dietrich Von Hildebrand wrote in his manifesto *In Defense of Purity* that the loose woman participates in a "significant squandering of self." He argued that her self disperses at the same rate as her lovers multiply. According to Hildebrand, when a man sleeps with a loose woman he enters a "mystery of a terrible sin," in which he is in danger of losing his soul. In this black-hearted woman's embrace, man is in the grip of a "diabolically evil lust."

Throughout patriarchal history the loose woman has had no loose man as a counterpart. Never has the promiscuous man been perceived as evil and dangerous the way the promiscuous woman has. Indeed, the promiscuous man has often been romanticized as a Don Juan, a Casanova. Today the modern high school slut still has no remotely comparable male parallel. As many girls I interviewed phrased it, "the girls are sluts, the boys are studs."

The Casanova breaks hearts but the loose woman wreaks a different kind of havoc. Seducing men into the darkness of their own chaotic lust, she can cause the purest love to fall apart. In the 1961 film *Splendor in the Grass*, the struggle for the soul of man between the good virgin and the evil whore is presented in bold, melodramatic strokes. Directed by Elia Kazan and based on a play by William Inge, *Splendor in the Grass* starred twenty-four-year-old Warren Beatty and a doe-eyed Natalie Wood. It tells the story of a football hero and an all-American girl who fall in love, only to see their love undermined by forces beyond their control, forces embodied by the town floozy, who cracks her gum and wears too much lipstick.

As the film opens, it's 1928 in Wichita, Kansas, and the American economy is booming. Beatty plays Bud, the young prince of the Stamper family. His father is the richest man in town, an oil tycoon who struck black gold. Big Daddy Stamper is a hard-drinking war hero with glassy eyes and a mean limp. He bosses the kids around and threatens them with disinheritance; he has so much money, he seems like a king.

On the other side of the tracks lives Deenie Loomis, played by Wood. Deenie's family is poor and they are barely holding on to their middle-class status. Her father is a wimpy man with a soft voice and a beleaguered expression. He has not triumphed during the triumph of capitalism. He is the kind of guy who will never find black gold no matter how hard he looks.

Deenie and Bud fall in love despite their class differences. They stare into each other's eyes, dizzy with hormones. They are beautiful creatures with all the world in front of them. The scenes between them, as Deenie tries to stay a virgin, are some of the greatest representations of sexual frustration ever put on screen.

At the heart of the drama, Bud becomes impatient with Deenie because she will never allow him past first base. Bud dreams of fourth base like his father wishes he would dream of Yale. But Deenie keeps pushing his hands away. Dreaming of sex with Deenie, Bud becomes more and more feverish: he can't control his temper, he can't eat or sleep. Finally, one night after dinner, Bud's father advises him, "There's always two kinds of girls, and us boys we'd never mention them in the same breath, but every now and then one of us would sneak off and we'd get steam out of our system."

On his father's advice, Bud gets the steam out of his system with the town's loose girl. He picks her up after a game and they make out savagely underneath a waterfall, accompanied by swelling music. The viewer knows without a doubt: this kiss with the loose girl is the end of purity.

Meanwhile at home Deenie learns it is unnatural for girls to feel aggressively sexual. Her mother, wearing a dusty dress and a spaced-out expression, tells her sex is only for procreation. "I only let your father touch me when it was for making you," she proclaims, as Deenie hovers on the edge of a nervous breakdown.

All around the characters there is a thick aura of anxiety. The anxiety is not only sexual but also historical: it's about the inability to maintain the purity of love but also about the inability to keep the prosperous times going. As Bud gives up on Deenie and finds release with the loose girl (who dresses like a flapper, as all the loose girls do in *Splendor in the Grass*), so too the economy collapses into depression. In this scenario, the crash of pure monogamous love is part of the same fragmentation that brings about the crash of the marketplace.

When Bud sleeps with the bad girl, he also ruins the possibility of a perfect future with Deenie. In the end, he gets married and has children, but the film makes clear that it is not a perfect family, not what he could've had with Deenie if only he had waited for her.

When Bud's father pulls him close and tells him about the "other kind" of girl, he unleashes the slut onto the world. He corrupts Bud by telling him a secret of masculinity that all boys must learn sooner or later: that some girls should be used for sex, other girls reserved for love. Both Bud's father and Deenie's mother take it upon themselves to tell their children about "that kind of girl."

The role the parents play in *Splendor in the Grass* illustrates the way the loose girl is not merely someone kids learn about from their peers; she's a lesson they learn within the family. She's an old wives' tale like the warning about what happens if you keep your eyes crossed for too long. She's an intractable superstitious lesson: "Don't write in red pen or you'll become a whore." Over time the terms and images used to evoke her change, but there's always some lexicon that addresses her, some system of warnings in place surrounding her. She might be called a floozy or a tramp or shopworn, but she is always here, always waiting on the other side of the tracks, hoping for a man who has too much steam in his system to come and knock on her door.

One of the oldest and most enduring terms used to condemn promiscuous women is "home wrecker." The phrase refers, of course, to the way the loose woman steals the husband away from the wife. When she steals him, the home falls apart; without him there to keep it together, the security of the family dissolves.

The home wrecker sleeps with men who are taken, and by sleeping with them she breaks a law of property. The home wrecker violates the boundary around the "taken" man. She behaves as if everyone belongs to her, when in fact no one belongs to her. Through her actions she undermines monogamy, makes men temporarily lose their honor and their senses, and makes them forget their priorities. She flouts the marriage union that has been built on a foundation of laws under the eyes of God. In marriage, the man and woman promise to cleave to each other, but then she, as they say, gets her claws into him.

In the home wrecker myth there are always terrible consequences of succumbing to her: lust renders the father, and by association his family, homeless, disowned, dispossessed. Because the father has been distracted by her, the seemingly intact walls of his home are reduced to dust. The fragmentation of his love undermines all that seemed rock solid. She is loose, and her influence loosens his hold on home.

A female who can create such damage has been invested with a great deal of power, since the wreckage she creates is no small thing—it is, to the contrary, permanent, lasting, and endlessly proliferating. Thus although the home wrecker is denigrated and diminished, spoken of as if she's somehow worthless, the continual assertion of her worthlessness masks a fear of her true, scaleless potential. She's a reminder of the fickle nature of sexual arousal, of the fact that anyone can be made a fool of by sex at any moment, anyone can find himself suddenly transformed back into a teenager.

Desire has the power to demolish the world, to crack every foundation. Pulling at the edges of our consciousness is an undeniable destructive dream, a temptation toward betrayal, toward the stranger, toward the foreign land far from home where no one holds you accountable and no one knows your name. The home wrecker embodies this dream of getting lost, of being set adrift. No wonder everyone is afraid of her.

Since the contempt for the home wrecker derives from the reverence for the home, how far she's cast out shifts in response to fluctuations in this broader faith. In the 1920s, as has been widely documented, girls who acted like home wreckers were in vogue. The flapper was the It Girl; she even made the cover of *Life* magazine in a famous cartoon by John Held Jr., and she was celebrated by Dorothy Parker ("Her manners cause a scene, / But there is no more harm in her / Than in a submarine"). This was a time when social conventions were being flouted, and the girl with red lipstick and an aggressive sexuality found a certain level of acceptance.

Whenever talk of free love arises, as it did in the twenties, the home wrecker is given a little more leeway. Yet even when "that kind of girl" is in vogue, there is always a healthy contempt for her, and this contempt comes to people as naturally as homesickness. It is the homesick imagination that vilifies and detests the home wrecker: hatred of her is fueled by a powerful nostalgia for an archetypal mother who keeps the home fires burning, a father who makes his family safe from the night. The root of "family" is the same as the root of the word "familiar"; when we grow homesick, we are tired of the strangeness of the world and we want familiarity back. The home wrecker brings about a sexual disorientation wherein it is impossible to make out the familiar landmarks of unconditional love.

The homesick longing for a changeless world that does not contradict itself persists over time. In millennial America there has been much talk about how the whole idea of home has changed as the nuclear family has been transformed. The rise of single mothers, gay and lesbian parents represented in sitcoms about the kid with two dads—all these new formulations of the family have for utopian progressives come to represent the complete restructuring of America itself. Zine writer David Grad has referred in his writings to "the impending extinction of the American family," an extinction he describes as having a revolutionary potential.

One would imagine at such a time, when the most basic structure of the family is being questioned, contempt for the home wrecker would be on the wane. But based on my interviews, this does not seem to be the case. The specter of the home wrecker is alive and well; she's as feared and hated as she ever was. In the hallways of high school, the girl who might steal boys away is still invested with a timeless evil; there's still an air of doom about her. Like the teenagers in *Splendor in the Grass*, kids still believe in pure love and the girl who trespasses on it.

When Karen Lehman and I drove around Andover Heights, we looked at the places where her mother had moved with her kids, following various fathers. Karen described her mother as pursuing a dream of home and of a family headed by a father, but it was not a dream her own children believed in. They saw the dad thing as a kind of pipe dream their mother kept succumbing to. Then everything turned into a soap opera, and the dad always left. By Dad number three, Karen and her brother basically saw dads as jokes, phenomenal absences.

Sometimes Karen thinks that if she'd had a father, things would have turned out all right. The nostalgia for a life with Father she never had exceeds and predates her; arguably, it is the nostalgia at the heart of patriarchy. There is a shimmering and appealing dream that Father will solve the sadness at the heart of the world, that Father will keep everyone safe even in snowstorms, that he will find you when you are lost in a dark wood. This is the nostalgia religion often draws on, and it's a nostalgia that Karen feels when we drive through Andover Heights. For Karen, this place is a minefield of lost fathers.

On right-wing radio, the disappearance of fathers is often identified as a sign of the decline of civilization. This is particularly true on the Dr. Laura show, which in 2001 draws a daily audience estimated at 18 million listeners. Dr. Laura's show is a prolonged lament about the decline of the nuclear family— she believes that the fractured family has brought civilization to the brink of Babylon. One of the ideas at the center of Dr. Laura's message is that since stay-at-home moms have disappeared from the scene, children have become increasingly violent and rootless. According to this argument, working women have brought about the proliferation of everything from school shootings to abortion, which Dr. Laura calls "sucking grandbabies down the sink."

Listen to Dr. Laura's program for any length of time, as

she talks about the good old days when "people didn't go to bed together at the drop of a hat" the way they do now, and one has to wonder about the story she's telling. There was, of course, never a time when people didn't act on the lust that threatens the family. And there was never a time when kids weren't violent, or when all mothers knew how to be good mothers and all fathers knew how to be good fathers.

Nevertheless the nostalgia for such a time fuels and energizes Dr. Laura's show. For Dr. Laura the decline of the family in our time has been the by-product of female selfishness. By not standing by their men, women have brought about the demise of the past good world, causing an epidemic of illegitimate children who feel an emptiness where the father should be. Dr. Laura has a litany of names for these women: "sluts" is the favorite and "pigs" is the second most common. According to Dr. Laura, feminists and proabortion activists are the greatest home wreckers of them all. She believes the desire for liberation expressed in the seventies was greedy, based on a wish to be able to do anything one wants without any consequences. When she talks about feminism, she talks about women who do not want to be real women and who are afraid of real men.

Dr. Laura's program has been a catalyst, spawning trends in return-to-modesty acolytes and born-again virgins. These women's movements claim that something is rotting in the state of womanhood, that a dangerous decay and corruption has been brought about by feminism and the aftereffects of the sexual revolution. In that revolution's wake, there has been a decline in morals: women don't say no anymore and they don't appreciate the virtues of being hard to get—they are too grasping, too busy talking about what they want. For Dr. Laura and her vast number of female followers the story goes like this: women are either mothers or sluts. There is no ambiguity, there is no middle region.

Roughly three-quarters of Dr. Laura's callers are women. These women talk about how they wish they were not so stupid; they wish they had never acted like selfish sluts; they wish they had seen the light and listened to her. And now, they ask, is it too late to change my ways?

The girls I interview seem to know intuitively that for many men, they represent the opposite of going home. They manifest a readiness to be cast out of the traditional love story, to be the girl under the waterfall Warren Beatty abandons with a sour look on his face. Kristen, twenty-two, told me: "I have been dating this guy for six months almost. He's thirty-one, and I really like him. But he seems to have this vision of me as this pure, untainted individual. I haven't told him any of this. I don't want to spoil it." Ever since her slut years, Kristen has felt that if she talks about her past with guys she's currently dating, they immediately start to look at her differently. Nancy, nineteen, said of her high school slut period: "It's still getting in my way. I can't trust men. Even men I love dearly." Nancy still feels a sense of vertigo whenever a man comes near her. She thinks of herself as someone who is constitutionally unable to have a normal, committed relationship. Many girls suspected that once they had been identified as home wrecker types, men would feel endangered by them.

These women had a palpable anxiety about what's called

in women's magazines "relationship potential." They proved that even in a postfeminist age, the old ideas of "that kind of girl" still hold sway in the imagination. Tonia, twenty-five, has just been through a divorce and she talks about her husband turning on her the way boys used to turn against her in high school—suddenly acting like she was contaminated. "He thought I was flirting with his best friend. It was like being in high school all over again."

For the former slut, the period of ostracism reemerges and separates her from being the type of girl who's marriage material. Surrounded by the mystique of her promiscuous past, she feels like the bride who shouldn't be allowed to wear white; her sins are so various and evident that there is no possibility of returning to her former state of purity. The institution of the nuclear family is ultimately the thing that is held up in judgment against her, the realm she cannot achieve because her rumored acts have exiled her from it.

In this way the girls I interviewed were not so far from the target audience of the 1967 *Seventeen Guide to Knowing Yourself,* which described the fast girl as someone a young male would decide "is not the kind of girl I want to be the mother of my children." The girls I interviewed still believed that there was something so unnatural about being the slut, it was enough to get them banished from family life altogether, from the exclusive club of mothers and wives.

In *Our Guys,* Bernard Lefkowitz described the little mothers as one of the most revered tribes at Glen Ridge. The tribe's name was a remarkable illustration of the way high school girls are still divided into categories of marriage material and non–marriage material based on whether they seem like the kind of girl who will procreate and be a good mother to children. If we need to revere mothers to keep the story of the West going, we also need to revile the home wrecker to keep our system of meanings in place. When women are divided into categories, the slut lives on the underside of mother reverence—she actually compels the reiteration of mother reverence. Just as in high school the slut delineates a boundary for girls and boys, beyond which one is a sexual freak, so too the home wrecker delineates the boundaries of the home. She's the reference point on the map. She is from the wrong side of the tracks and hence indicates the location of the right side of the tracks. When we arrive in her neighborhood, we know we've gone too far.

Exiled from the motherly, bridal role in the nuclear family narrative, the girl who has been deemed the slut develops a sense that she is an outsider, that she belongs elsewhere. For many girls I interviewed, this sense of otherness expressed itself in their often feeling "like a man." One twenty-three-year-old described herself as "macho and heartless. I can fuck 'em and chuck 'em, no problem!" Another told me about how she just goes after the conquest, then forgets about all the "BS girl stuff" afterward. A lot of girls wished they had been born boys so instead of being singled out as sluts, they would've been revered as studs.

For girls to talk about feeling "like a man" was another way of talking about being completely alienated from the sexual story they found themselves surrounded by. It was a way of proclaiming their place outside the feminine—even though they were born girls, they didn't feel like true girls. It was also a way of reckoning with the idea of themselves as aggressive sexual agents, instead of passive little mothers waiting in the wings, who have sex only for the right reasons.

Feeling like a man meant feeling like an explorer, an aggressor, one who overtakes territories and claims them as one's own. To be a macho "heartless fuck" was also to imagine oneself as a boy who could be forgiven, who could forgive himself. For these girls, if their sins were sins of gender, maybe they had been born into the wrong gender—maybe they had been born into the wrong body altogether.

Kids inherit these stories of whores and sluts and their diabolical potential. When one is in the midst of these stories they seem as inescapable as the weather, and only as one gets older is it possible to sometimes see the contradictions. The archetype of the slut had already taken root in my mind by the time I arrived in high school. I was only waiting for a manifestation of something I had always intuitively known about. I knew Anna Wanna was there before she arrived.

When I finally laid eyes on her, I was more than ready to hate her—I was primed for it. As she sashayed down the hallway, acting like she was more than us, I felt a stifled and intrigued resentment. Part of me wished I could be her. I wished my phone was ringing off the hook with the calls of dirty-minded boys. But at home my phone was silent.

I would look at Anna Wanna and I would feel my stomach churning with a jealous wonder: How did this girl end up at the center of sex and boys, when I felt like boys were always eluding me? What was this amazing world she was in the middle of, while I read about Shaun Cassidy in *Tiger Beat* and ordered a life-size poster of his dimpled face for my door? I was so bored that I wanted to be shopworn. I hated her for the kisses I believed she had stolen from me and from all of us unremarkable girls, sitting on the sidelines in the cafeteria dutifully eating our lunches. My resentment toward Anna was different from the resentment of girls whose boyfriends she'd stolen; since I had no boyfriends, there was no physical person she could steal from me. But I still felt she was taking something away.

Boys use the slut to get the steam out of their systems. But she is never really out of the system; she is intrinsic to it. She is so embedded in the stories we tell one another at home that if we were ever to stop telling stories of her, the family itself would change. If we were no longer threatened by the home wrecker, the home itself would be different from the home we imagined for so long. And we bring these beliefs out of the home into the world, into the school where other kids swarm, everyone flush with the belief that the girl is out there somewhere, and she needs to be named.

6

THEMES OF ISOLATION

The woman who thinks in isolation
thinks evil thoughts.

—Malleus Maleficarum

In a biography of singer Janis Joplin called *Scars of Sweet Paradise*, Alice Echols traces the way the high school slut story affected and transformed her subject. Growing up in Port Arthur, Texas, Janis was an awkward girl with bad acne, liberal politics, and a weird laugh. At Thomas Jefferson High School she developed a reputation for being loose; as Echols writes,

> What really sealed Janis's fate as a social untouchable was her growing reputation as the school slut. At some point in her junior year, Janis felt compelled to appear

promiscuous. Among her friends there is no consensus on how Janis came by her new role. It may have developed because word had it that Janis was tired of being ignored and threw herself into the one activity that was sure to get a Port Arthur girl talked about. Whatever the reason, Janis certainly knew it wouldn't take much to earn a bad reputation at TJ High. By her senior year, the rumors were flying that Janis Joplin read pornography and was making out with guys right and left.

Joplin endured acts of cruelty that echoed the testimonies of the girls I interviewed: kids threw pennies at her and spat in her face. Even to hang out with her brought about what Echols calls "weirdness by association." Eventually Janis found a certain degree of community among the beatniks and, later, the hippies, but she was always tormented by a fabulous loneliness, by the sense that she was an outcast. It's possible to detect this desolation at the core of her burning, reckless voice.

Joplin's loneliness remained the one constant of her life, and her sense of being alone and apart has become part of her iconography. She is often represented as a woman surrounded by an impenetrable static field of sadness. She has been widely interpreted by rock critics and fans as an outsider, a freak of pop culture. As Echols vividly renders it, Joplin's slut period was a key factor in her persistent, destructive feelings of being the wrong sort of person, the wrong sort of woman. To combat this, Joplin developed a swagger and a cigarette voice; she became a character, a tough girl, a ball buster. She studied the recordings of Bessie Smith and pushed her voice to sound as strong as Bessie's did. She became the loudest girl in town. Many girls I interviewed also grew loud inside their reputations; they manufactured an aura of imperviousness and outrageousness so that, as Margaret, twenty-two, said, "no one could fuck with me." Developing wild personas, girls embraced their infamy, relishing the ability to shock and to drown everybody else out. The loud persona camouflaged a deeper silence; it was also a form of rebellion and an offensive action in the face of a hostile environment.

Although none of the girls I interviewed had achieved the celebrity of Joplin, they still very often behaved like famous people. They had felt the eyes of the crowd on them and had become the object of tabloid-style gossip. It was as if a spotlight were shining down on them. As sixteen-year-old Elaine describes it, "I felt like I was in the freak booth at the circus!"

The fame of the slut works to set her apart. She is always wondering if people know who she is, and if they do, what they want from her. "They" could be boys or girls, parents or teachers. Like rock stars, high school sluts are in the grip of the crowd's voracious dream.

It would be a mistake to tell this story as if the girls designated as sluts are the only kids who feel like outsiders in high school. In many ways, feeling outside and not all there is a universal element of adolescence. Walking down the hallway at Calhoun, I could see loneliness everywhere: there was the girl in a cape and black boots huddled in a corner; the not-quite-popular girl with her desperate, trying-to-belong laugh; the boy with a Motorhead T-shirt who looked about ten years too old for this place. All these kids had a furtive, desperate look that seemed to signify loneliness.

The inherent loneliness of high school was illuminated in the contemporary mainstream media for a brief time after the Columbine massacre. Investigations into the phenomenon of cliques and how they work to isolate kids occurred in the aftermath. In 2001, after another Columbine-style shooting at Santana High School in suburban San Diego, California, social psychologist Dr. Elliot Aaronson was interviewed by the *New York Times*. A researcher into the phenomenon of teenagers' tribal behavior, Aaronson painted a harsh picture for the reporter. He explained: "It's the cliquish atmosphere of rejection and humiliation that makes a very significant minority of students, I would say 30 to 40 percent of them, very, very unhappy. If kids at the top of the pyramid start calling a kid a nerd, then the kids in the second tier of cliques tease him because that's one way of identifying with the powerful group. Next thing you know everybody's teasing him. . . . When exclusion takes the form of taunting and humiliation, you're beginning to sow the seeds of violence."

Aaronson described a tier system in which the top of the pyramid belongs to the most popular kids. Yet really the metaphor is more accurate if the pyramid is reversed: in the merciless popularity contest that is high school, the layers get smaller and smaller until there is only one person alone at the tip of the pyramid. In the popular crowd, there is always someone sitting next to you at the cafeteria table, passing the rumor on to you, whispering into your ear, or tugging your shirt. But the further you get from popularity, traveling through various levels of unpopularity in the direction of ostracism, the more the specter of your own outcast self starts to shadow your soul. The one thing you do not want to be is without friends, cut out from the grapevine—especially in contemporary America, with the ghosts of Columbine at the forefront of consciousness. The lesson of Columbine is: if you are alone, if you are a freak, you might be a psychotic, too.

One of the most persistent forms of ostracism, outside the slut story, is to label someone a fag. Boys who are deemed fags or sissies undergo a relentless taunting that is similar to what the slut endures; like the girls I interviewed, boys who are deemed the fag find themselves at the receiving end of unpredictable violence and amazingly detailed rumors fabricated from a weird collective sexual ignorance. A gay man I know who grew up in Spokane, Washington, remembers the day the jocks threw him through a plate glass window.

Like sluts, fags are ostracized because of what the mob believes they have been doing in the darkness—there is something wrong with the way both the fag and the slut want to be touched and want to be entered. Their desires are deviant. Both the fag and the slut feel an isolation and alienation within school that has a different texture from ordinary teenage alienation; as sexual *and* social outcasts, they are doubly alienated.

Outlandish, archaic fears rise to the surface of the hormonal teenage mind—the fear of sexual disorientation, of a desire that could explode the family and wreck the home. As sexual freaks, the slut and the fag are renamed by the kids around them, their subjectivities erased by a myth of deviance. Kids turn the slut or the fag into an alien being, even as they themselves are in the grip of a common and well-documented phase of moody teenage alienation. They pick him or her out to be even more of a stranger than they already feel themselves to be.

Once kids find themselves on the receiving end of slut or fag ostracism, they lose their ability to predict what violence the day might hold within it. They cannot know, for example, if they will make it through classes without incident, or if they will go sailing through a window at the hands of the mob. The mob is in control. The mob descends, riding on a wave of astonishing certainty.

Traditional developmental narratives describe coming of age as a gradual solidifying and strengthening of the subject—the dawning realization of the self. But the girl chosen as the high school slut experiences coming of age not as the dawning of self-possession and subjectivity but as a darkening loss of self and complete objectification. For many of the girls I interviewed, by the time they emerged from the slut period they had almost no sense of self left at all.

The more infamous a girl becomes as the high school years press on and her reputation flourishes, the more she feels like she does not have any core connection to her own name. As with the rock star whose fans claim to know him better than he knows himself, the crowd is utterly convinced they can see into her. The crowd's conviction loosens her identity from its moorings. Her subjectivity is smeared and muddied, crowded out by voices. Any truth of herself that she might try to present to the jury of her peers is canceled out by other testimonies. Everyone swears they know what she has been doing: giving blow jobs for cigarettes, saying yes to the whole football team. When they say her first and last name, their voices drip with sarcasm.

This is a surreal experience that is difficult to overcome; it's not a run-of-the-mill teen trauma that can be easily integrated into a forward-moving logic of dawning adulthood. Exposed at a formative time to graphic sexual humiliation, insurmountable power imbalances, and acts of pure hatred, the girls deemed high school sluts witness a regressive underside to the coming-of-age drama—they are in some sense human sacrifices of this drama. The slut, like the fag, is pushed out into the unconscious territory at precisely the moment when pleasure is beginning to be regulated and administered.

Adolescence is normally the point when signs appear on bedroom doors: KEEP OUT, KNOCK BEFORE YOU ENTER. It's the era of the new driver's license, a piece of plastic that allows a young person to drive outside the boundaries parents have set, out into what Bruce Springsteen romanticized as "the darkness at the edge of town." For girls who are the slut, the privacy that KEEP OUT signs symbolize cannot be attained: the door can never be closed to the bedroom; the darkness on the edge of town where she's not afraid or ashamed keeps eluding her. There is nowhere to go where the gaze and the whisper do not follow her. Anything she does could be written on the bathroom wall the next day. She could drive as far out of town as possible, hang out with kids from a completely different place, and the rumors would still somehow trickle back. "I even switched schools, trying to start over," one girl explained. "And in the new school everyone was saying I had crabs. They had heard it from someone who heard it from someone."

The former high school slut fears, above all, being objectified again. And since my interviews were in many ways a process of objectification, of seeing a girl not as an individual but as part of a continuum and an archetype, the encounter was sometimes difficult to navigate. Was I engaged in one more form of writing what I wanted to about her, only this time not on the bathroom wall?

In a book called *The Journalist and the Murderer,* Janet Malcolm writes:

> Every journalist who is not too stupid or too full of himself to notice what is going on knows that what he does is morally indefensible. He is a kind of confidence man, preying on people's vanity, ignorance, loneliness, gaining their trust and betraying them without remorse. Like the credulous widow who wakes up one day to find the charming young man and all her savings gone, so the consenting subject of a piece of nonfiction writing learns— when the article or book appears—*his* hard lesson.

Malcolm's book centers on the relationship between convicted killer Jeffrey MacDonald and journalist Joe McGinnis. It's an inspired deconstruction of the promises a journalist makes to a subject in order to get a story out of him. I didn't read Malcolm's book until after I had conducted my interviews, but when I did, I looked back and saw myself reflected in what she said. I saw the way I was trying to build an atmosphere of trust so that my subjects would come forward with their stories. I was trying to convince the girls I interviewed that I had their best interests at heart. In my attempt to bring them close enough to record what they were saying, I employed the well-worn feminist language of "getting your story told."

Needless to say, a lot of these girls did not trust me. Why should they? There was nothing in the interaction to guarantee my veracity, my sympathy. I was just a girl with an earnest look and an earnest voice, the kind of girl who played violin in high school and probably passed on rumors. As the stories emerged, it was clear that many girls felt ambivalent about the act of telling—they moved back and forth between feeling that they should talk about this and feeling that they shouldn't. Was talking about it one more way of igniting the rumors? If they talked about being the slut, would they once again become her? Because of this hesitance and mistrust, the promise of anonymity was useful when I tried to get them to talk about what had happened back then or what was still happening. The promise of anonymity was a promise that, for once, you could be anyone; you could disappear, you could slip out from underneath your name.

Tricia, twenty-two, was reassured when I told her that I would alter her story so that no one could recognize her. I promised to change or blur details for her, similar to what's seen on television when a digital screen is placed over the face and the voice is hollowed out by sound equipment. Yet despite my promises and her initial enthusiasm, Tricia remained guarded about her story and ultimately put it away, refused to verbalize it any further, at a point when I thought I was going to break her story open.

In a series of phone interviews she tells me about growing up. "My dad is a truck driver and my mom is a housewife. I went to a public school with a graduating class of about seventy-five kids." Tricia developed breasts and hips early and she soon became infamous in such a small school. In junior high, "On a daily basis kids would be saying I slept with someone. This was in sixth grade. Kids in the hallway, seventh- and eighth-graders, would say, 'Hey, there's the slut.' A group of guys would walk me home, expecting something."

Tricia felt that she had earned her reputation through her actions. "Until I was sixteen I was really, really sexually active. I thought that the only way to get attention from men was to have sex with them." She looks at herself back then and sees a girl out of control. Everyone knew, everyone spoke of it. There was only one bar in town, and her father heard about her sexual exploits from the regulars there, who had heard about her from their own sons. "Yeah, my dad would be drinking, and this barfly would be telling him about how I'd lost my virginity to his son."

The claustrophobic nature of Tricia's story piques my curiosity. I ask if I can fly out, rent a car, and go on a tour of her town with her. I imagine that since she has told her story to me once, she will want to keep telling it. At first she seems enthusiastic, and we have a phone conversation in which we start to figure out schedules and logistics—when she might have time to spend a weekend away from college and drive down into the heart of her past with me.

Tricia initially called me after a friend talked her into it—a gay male friend who read "Savage Love" and had seen the way she agonized over her past memories. He'd told her, "Maybe you need to get this out." At first she believed that telling her story would allow her to get over it. But she gradually became suspicious of the talking cure.

Over the course of a few weeks, it becomes more and more difficult to get Tricia on the phone. She doesn't return my messages, and when I do reach her, she sounds slightly annoyed as soon as she realizes it's me once again. She says, "I can't talk about this right now, could you call back tomorrow, or next weekend?" I realize my field trip out to see her isn't going to happen. She tells me, "I've decided I don't want to talk about this with you or relive it. I think it's best just to get beyond it."

I try to coax her back out, but she won't be swayed. In the futile effort of trying to change her mind, I am pulling her in the direction of the small town with the one school where her name was on every boy's tongue. This is a place she doesn't want to go. It's a freeway exit she doesn't want to take in a stranger's rented car.

There are ways in which I, as a journalist, appear to be in the same tribe as the friend in the cafeteria who betrayed Karen at the Catholic school in Andover Heights. This friend listened intently to Karen talk about her beloved blue-eyed man as if everything Karen said mattered, and then she went out into the school yard and completely distorted the story, turning it into a freak show. For all these girls know, I am just like the girl in Karen's story who sits down at the cafeteria table, as nice as can be, and asks to hear the story of the past.

Like the girl who acts like a friend but is not a friend, I must be treated with suspicion. I could be putting on an act of kindness while all the time really plotting to steal the story and set it down in my own language, use it for my own purposes.

Karen talked about how there was a moment when she needed to "close a door in [her] mind" on her slut experience—to try to forget it, bury it, not allow it to keep surfacing in her every waking moment. At various times in her life she did forget, and sometimes even thought she was free of it. But the story always came back, and when she talks to me about what happened back then, she says, "I think this is something I need to do."

Karen is intensely verbal and expressive, her words fill the air and displace her past with their noise. Other girls did not choose to engage in this act of displacement. In the space of four hours, I received two messages from Lainie, a twenty-three-year-old Midwesterner. She spoke in a breathy, panicky voice and described her years in high school when kids called her slut and never called her by her real name. "In my own mind I was perfect, Sandra Dee," she says, but to the other kids, "I was the dirty slut." As with many other girls Lainie describes a bad home life—parents who kicked her out, a pattern of exile.

In her message Lainie expresses a desire to talk about what happened. She wants to talk about the injustices of the hallway, the weird rumors of parties where she allowed boys to "put bottles and pens inside me." But four hours later she leaves another message. She says she's feeling strange about calling me, that she has started to worry about the possibility of me calling back when her fiancé is home because she doesn't "want him to know anything about this." She gives a series of specific directions about when to call and what to say into the machine if she isn't home. The determination has disappeared from her voice.

I try to call Lainie for weeks but the phone rings into what sounds like emptiness. The sound of the ringing phone without any answer or even an answering machine strikes me as sad; I am convinced that I have lost something. Just as in my failed pursuit of Tricia, when I call Lainie and get no answer I feel spurned. I feel like she backed away from the story and buried it, when what I want to do is get down into the center of it and unbury it.

This feeling of regret about Lainie's untold story is not rational, of course. I never even talked to Lainie, so I am not sure if she has decided to back away from the slut story or if she had just called me on a lark and then had other, more pressing things to think about. I project onto the emptiness at the other end of the phone line what feminists sometimes call the silence of history. One girl doesn't answer the phone; a message cannot be sent. Since Lainie is only thirty seconds of a voice, an outline of a form, it is easy to project a multitude of girls onto her. She loses her particularity and becomes a sign of everything that hasn't been said. She becomes a symbol of the self-imposed isolation I have encountered throughout my interviews. The static on the other end of the telephone line takes on melancholy proportions in my mind. Like an overwhelmed high school counselor, looking around at the lonely kids in the hallway, I cannot help but wonder: What can I do to get through to them? What can I do to get them to open up? Don't I seem like a person who should be trusted?

When a girl has been labeled the slut, other kids don't want to get near her. The promiscuous reputation overcomes a girl's experience like a flu that refuses to leave. Both girls and boys protect themselves from her as if she is contagious, sometimes even washing their hands after touching her. Like the "girl germs" games young kids play, the slut is considered contaminated: don't get too close or her pollution will attach itself to your skin.

Slut rumors often revolve around venereal diseases: in my interviews, girls recounted rumors of crabs, AIDS, herpes, and syphilis. The specter of venereal disease plays into a wider notion that the slut's very presence represents and embodies sickness—both physical sickness and a vague soul sickness. Like the fear of witches that led to the burning of young women at the stake in 1600s Salem, the slut story relies on the notion that there is something insidious in the slut's existence and that if she is not ostracized, her poisonous influence will spread.

So kids keep themselves apart from the slut, create a safe distance. Even if boys claim to have slept with her, they are never really "with" her; to show any loyalty to her would be to make themselves contaminated too. Girls who at one time might have been friends with the slut recede as her reputation grows; they need to be careful how they associate with her or they will be thought of as sluts along with her. To get too near is dangerous: kids do not want their names spoken in the same breath as hers. Her reputation is transmissible if one isn't careful.

Crawling with germs and soul sickness, the slut finds herself enclosed, living in a kind of quarantine. Nobody can come in and she cannot get out. She does not know other girls who are in a similar isolation; the nature of the isolation is that it appears she is the only one: she's doing things in a way no other girls do things, she's an island of sickness unto herself.

Thus, while in high school there are bands of freaks and small contingents of fags, a remarkable element of the slut story is how all these girls felt totally alone within it. Even though they were all speaking to me of a shared experience, they had no sense of its commonality. Indeed, the idea that other girls might feel this too was foreign to them; when I would say it was happening to many others, they would invariably express surprise. The slut story happens to multitudes, to a vast sisterhood of women, but the way the system of quarantine works, a girl can only see it happening to herself.

When Tricia decided she didn't want to talk about the slut period anymore, what she said was, "I was really starting to feel healthy. Talking about this made me feel unhealthy." At twenty-two, the metaphors of health and sickness still surround the slut story for her; the slut is still perceived as the sick version of the self, the piece of the past that should remain in quarantine.

*　　　*　　　*

A March 1999 *Cosmo* magazine survey asked readers: "Should you reveal how many people you've slept with?" Melvin, twenty-eight, a veterinarian, writes, "Ladies, lie with a low number or else we'll end up imagining all sorts of sick scenarios involving you and the college swim team." Cynthia, twenty-eight, a lab technician, says, "Definitely tell your partner, but if the number is more than ten, lie. That seems to be the magic number in men's heads that turns fabulous girl-friends into trampy ho-bags."

The *Cosmo* reader is advised to lie about her past in order to avoid appearing contaminated. She should revise her list of lovers to make it seem harmless, unthreatening. Her past needs to be cleansed and purified—ideally she will seem to have no history at all. History-free, she makes the most fabulous girlfriend of all.

The idea that femininity itself is a culture of lying, forgetting, and erasure was something explored by Adrienne Rich in her seminal 1975 essay "Women and Honor: Some Notes on Lying." Working in a fragmented style somewhere between a journal entry and a manifesto, Rich writes:

> The woman who tells lies in her personal relationships may or may not plan or invent her lying. She may not even think of what she is doing in a calculated way.
>
> The liar often suffers from amnesia. Amnesia is the silence of the unconscious.
>
> The liar lives in fear of losing control. She cannot even desire a relationship without manipulation, since to be vulnerable to another person means for her loss of control.

Rich viewed women in their lying state as living in a world of self-estrangement and self-alienation. She argued that there was a true, buried story beneath the illusory world of femininity, and this might be the key to liberation. Rich drew from her own experience as a white suburban house-wife who later came out as a lesbian; she saw her attempt to be a good wife as an elaborate lie through which she protected herself from coming out of the closet.

To a writer like Rich, stirring up trouble in the seventies, it seemed that many women were to some extent hiding in a closet within patriarchy, afraid to walk out into the main house and stake their claim in the fight for space. By lying about who they were and their own desires, women hid from the realities of powerlessness and oppression. As a key influence on what came to be called the consciousness-raising movement, Rich argued that all of this willed forgetting was a form of remaining semiconscious.

Interviewing girls at the turn of the millennium, I could not help but think of Rich's amnesiac female and how the things she has tried to forget inevitably rush forward into consciousness. For so many of these girls, hiding, burying, or trying to downplay the sexual head trip they had been through only increased its power in their minds. The more they tried to build a wall between themselves and the slut, to keep themselves away from her and to outgrow her, the more curious they became about what was on the other side.

When a girl is faced with a wall beyond which it seems she cannot go, she has a few ways of trying to address the problem. For some girls it was a matter of backing away from the whole thing, trying to find another route through the maze of her life, a route that did not end up facing the wall. For others it was a matter of pulling the wall apart piece by piece, carefully examining the bricks from which it was built. And then there were girls who seemed prepared to demolish all walls and reduce them to rubble. These were the tough girls, the intimidating hellions, the girls who acted like rock stars.

In *Scars of Sweet Paradise,* Janis Joplin emerges as a woman whose voice tore holes in history. By straining her voice to its lowest and loudest reaches, by roaring out into the emptiness, Joplin broke through the silence that surrounded her and many women of her generation. For her legions of still devoted female fans, it was as if Joplin had said, *See, you thought there was a wall, but there was nothing there.*

In the course of my interviews I met many girls who similarly approached the world as if they could tear it down with a glare, a voice, a defiant and tough resilience. Many of these girls identified their ostracism as the seed of the courage they now felt coursing through them; it was as if being the slut released them from a femininity as seemingly inescapable as Alcatraz. Now that they had endured femininity's hell and come out the other side, surely they could endure anything, right?

Marie, eighteen, talks like a girl who has been through the ringer and seen it all. She is a rocker who blasts her eardrums out at shows. She has a low cigarette voice and a glare that could take out an army. She describes the beginning of her ostracism to me: "This was in eighth grade. I was going out with this guy I didn't know well. I broke up with him and he had this vengeance toward me. And I was having a lot of problems anyway, so kids thought I was a weirdo. I was really into drugs. My mom's a drug abuser and my stepdad's an alcoholic and my brother uses drugs a lot too. I was smoking weed and whatever else, and then I started shooting heroin."

The fact that she was a heroin ghost added to the slut rumors that built around Marie; it added to the aura of contamination surrounding her. People said she had AIDS, that her mother was a prostitute, "all this crap." The stories didn't let up for years, even after Marie went clean and sober. "When I wore a turtleneck to school one day, everyone said I was covering up hickeys."

Marie tells another story of forgetting: of her mom and stepdad forgetting about her as they floated down the addict's river Lethe. "I have grown up fast. I had to. When I was younger I got myself up to go to school, I got myself dinner, I went to bed, and my mom would come home and I'd wake up the next morning. Either she'd be in bed still dressed from the day before or she'd be passed out somewhere with vomit on the floor and I would have to clean it up."

Eventually Marie's mom went to a clinic to get sober, and moved Marie in with her friends' parents, Christian people who talked about God a lot. If at first it seemed like a new beginning, after a while Marie started to feel homesick. She wanted to get back to her mom. "I didn't belong there," she says. Marie's mother emerged from rehab clean and full of confidence; she and Marie moved away from the stepdad. But the recovery was short, the promises empty. "She tried, but some things don't work out." The good mother-daughter act didn't seem to be working for either of them. The stepdad came back. Marie is now starting to wonder if it's time to cut ties with her mother. When I talk to her she has just found her first apartment and is waiting to sign the lease.

Marie wears a leather jacket, her black hair is streaked with magenta. She says that after having been the school slut "for so fucking long," she now marches down the hallway in her combat boots and says, *"Fuck yourself,"* if anyone whispers anything at her. Once she kissed a girl on the mouth just to freak everyone out; another time she heard an outrageous thousand-in-one-night blow job rumor and said, "Yeah, I did it. *So what!"* These days, Marie revels in her notorious corruption, thinks of it as a kind of freedom. "I don't care what they say about me," she says, "because I know what's true in my mind." She acts like she is not exiled, like the world belongs to her. She walks so confidently in her boots, causing tremors in the ground beneath her feet. She presents herself as a girl who has crawled up out of the underworld, who has found her way through the isolation and the drugged dreams, and who will soon be living in her own heroic apartment. It is a way of coping, this tough act. It's a start.

7

THE CRUELTY OF GIRLS

CREATE LOVE NOT WHORES

—Banner at a feminist demonstration
outside the 1968 Miss America Pageant

If the slut is widely seen as a stock character in a testos-terone-fueled drama, if she has long been considered part of the boys-will-be-boys culture of high school, she's also a key character in girls' coming of age and sexual awakening. She distracts girls just as she does boys. She is just as much a part of their becoming, their hormonal fever. The passion that surrounds her, the sense of electricity and turn-on and contempt, is something girls partake in, too.

But if she makes girls' blood rush, it's not a sexual rush—at least it's not perceived or accepted as such. For boys, contempt for the slut is intermingled with desire, while for girls there is no pleasure they seek from her, there is no moment in the darkness they seek with her, in which they might act out the motions of love. Boys can foresee a sexual moment when they might ask the slut for forgiveness, but for girls forgiveness is not part of the picture and they react to her with a more straightforward, virulent negativity. Girls manifest a verbal and physical hostility toward the slut that is remarkable in its focused intensity. They ambush the slut in parking lots, whisper threats over telephone wires, and wait for her in the bathroom with fists clenched. Although warning pamphlets about sexual harassment in schools focus on acts perpetrated by boys, girls also harass one another. Girls are predators, too.

Patty, a fifteen-year-old from North Carolina, says, "The girls are doing most of it. They are the main ones. They're vicious!" Susan, twenty-five, agrees: "Boys would run their mouths, say they had sex with you, but it wasn't so much to malign you as it was to build his own image among his friends. The really vicious ones were the girls. They said awful things about you with no other aspiration but to hurt you personally." Meagan, nineteen, saw the rumors begin with an ex-boyfriend, but once girls heard the rumors about her, they believed the stories even more fervently than the boys did. "I lost my oldest friends because they believed the lies!" she says. Meagan describes a swift and lasting ostracism: she was erased from her friends' list of invitations, kicked out of the inner circle cafeteria table.

Trying to protect their boys from being seduced by the slut, girls warn her to stay away. Because she behaves like a girl without boundaries, they warn her about the lines she'd better not cross. *You stay away from my boyfriend, or else! You have been warned!* Some version of these threats was repeatedly aimed at the girls I interviewed. If the slut disobeyed and flirted with boys she had been ordered not to flirt with, the drama escalated. If she touched the wrong boy's shoulder, she could expect swift retaliation—new rumors, new threats, a shove with an even greater force of hatred behind it.

The rumors girls spread about the slut are essentially the same as the rumors boys spread, the train job being the most popular. But as one girl told me who remembered spreading rumors about the blow job queen, "I thought a blow job was, like, literally blowing on the head of a guy's penis." Earlier I discussed how girls have so little access to pornography that their sexual imaginations do not have much of a visual element. They are not quite sure what a blow job is, since they have not seen it in porno movies. Additionally, girls do not tend to have graphic conversations about sex the way boys do; they speak in terms of *Did you . . . ? Did you . . . ?* Thus the slut and her rumored acts exist in an elliptical darkness; her techniques are a mystery.

Faced with this mystery and with no way to alleviate it, girls lash out. Unable to either touch the slut or visualize her in action, they get panicky and their whispers become more and more urgent, full of thwarted, explosive energy.

Girls hate the slut because she is a story they are not allowed in on. The ways boys talk about the slut, about having a piece of her and what she was like—these conversations lead into rooms that girls cannot enter. Angry that they are not the center of attention, girls talk about how much they hate the way boys look at the slut. Indeed, the shifting of a boy's gaze away from a girlfriend toward the slut was often cited in my interviews as the beginning of girl hatred. When I asked one girl why she thought the girls came to hate her, she said, "Pure and simple. They hated the way their boyfriends looked at my tits."

Feminist theorist Luce Irigaray has argued that female coming of age is the process of realizing you live beneath the "male gaze." But the slut takes the gaze away—she steals it when she walks down the hall looking the way she looks. She distracts the attention of the male and takes the light of his stare onto herself. Girls feel adrift when his gaze has disappeared, and they'll do anything, even issue cryptic threats in late-night phone calls, just to get his stare turned back in their direction.

Although girls reassure one another that the slut is not someone a guy would want as a girlfriend, not the long-term type, her presence still makes them feel as if some space is being taken away, as if she is an invading force they must contain or erase before she takes over completely.

What atmosphere, what emotional climate, would cause girls to believe so fervently that the slut must be ostracized? The girls I interviewed often cited an environment of boy craziness as the background for the girl-on-girl slut wars— that giddy psychosis of crushes, the endless dating talk of girls, the thing that makes female fans scream for boy bands like they are being tortured. Boy craziness can bring about a powerful eclipse of reason, more powerful than drugs or hypnosis. It's like the adrenaline rush that gives a mother the strength to lift a car off her child—it can make a girl capable of anything.

The high school hallway is a reflection of the patriarchal world, and boy craziness is one more expression of the story in which the male is central, the hero. Girls call cute boys "gods"; they overvalue boys to the point that the whole high school economy threatens to fall apart. Girls with boyfriends are more valuable than girls without; girls with powerful boyfriends are powerful in relation, like politicians' wives. From the first day of school girls struggle to figure out how they fit into the boy story, the love story, the story of prom night and high heels and evening gowns, long soap opera kisses, fireworks in the blood. *He kissed my hand, and I swear I will never wash that hand again!*

In many ways, boy-crazy girls are a tribe unto themselves; they have their own language, their own rituals, their own superstitions and bizarre customs. Teen girls' magazines are the holy books of this tribe. *Seventeen, Young Miss,* and *Cosmo Girl* instruct the boy-crazy girl how to handle her frazzled state of mind: she should make sure she always looks cute by dieting, taking care of her skin, and wearing the latest fashions. She should make sure she learns how to meet the right boy, who is not going to use her, and she should study the details of the personal lives of her favorite boy band. The prototypical boy-crazy girl has a life-size picture of a teen hunk on her bedroom wall; she writes him letters on pink flowery stationery; she falls asleep with cucumber slices affixed to her eyes.

Statistics hint at one possible cause of boy craziness: sexuality researchers have found that many girls do not learn to masturbate to climax until they are twenty-one or twenty-two. Maybe with no form of release the pressure of desire gives way to a kind of dementia. Girls become unhinged, unmoored. They have no idea how to calm themselves down.

Julie Matthews, thirty, vividly remembers her boy-crazy high school days—how she was so worked up about sex she needed to smoke pot during lunch period just to be able to catch her breath. Julie's blond Farrah Fawcett hair and pretty face made her popular among the boys. She was never called a slut, never disrespected; people treated her like a goddess. "I was having sex with tons of guys," she says, "but I got away with it."

Julie grew up in a small town in rural Massachusetts where the mall and the woods were the only places to go. Everyone listened to Jethro Tull and smoked joints in the shade behind the school. Thinking back, Julie expresses disbelief at what a "little bitch" she was: crawling out her bedroom window in the middle of the night, stealing her parents' car keys, telling off her mother in streams of curses.

If Julie remembers getting away with her promiscuous behavior, she also remembers the one girl who did not get away with anything, a girl who was held captive by the rumors Julie and her friends spread. This girl was Suzanne Smith, and early in tenth grade, she was designated the school slut.

"If you asked anyone who the slut of our high school was back then, I guarantee you they would say Suzanne. But before we all decided she was a slut, Suzanne and I were best friends. We cruised the mall together. We both played like tough girls, but she was tougher, more confident in her beauty and sexuality. We wrote pages of notes to each other, always signed 'Balloon Sisters Forever.' This was accompanied by a drawing of two attached, smiling balloons, the point being if one popped and lost its air, the other died."

Julie and Suzanne's closeness proved transitory. Between ages thirteen and fourteen, as junior high became high school, their connection dissolved into static. As they entered adolescence and the boy-crazy stage, as they crossed over into this economy where girls have greater or lesser value based on their proximity to the slut, Julie and Suzanne grew apart. Julie jettisoned Suzanne as Suzanne's slutty reputation solidified.

Rumors had been building around Suzanne but Julie tried to ignore them at first. She was reluctant to ostracize someone she had known longer than she could remember, until one rumor emerged that she couldn't ignore. The rumor, which gave Julie a kind of amnesia about the friendship, described a night in a bedroom called "force five." In an e-mail letter, Julie recounts the force five legend:

One night at the beginning of sophomore year Suzanne called me and told me a story that became part of the big rumor of the school: "I went to a party at Rob Brown's house last night," she said, "and the weirdest thing is I woke up today and my underwear was on backwards!"

They called it "Force Five." Rob says she just started to pass out and while she was making out with one guy she began to put on a show for them. They all did it to her. When they were through, they cleaned her up, got her dressed and dropped her off on her doorstep.

After hearing this story I quickly, instinctively began

to reject Suzanne and listened to all the boys' stories with an almost sympathetic ear. Suzanne and I grew apart. She became even slinkier and scarier to me, a dark slutty version of her old self. With black eyeliner accentuating her slitted eyes, long feathered hair, and tight clothing, she was hot stuff for the boys to ponder. Girlfriends of ours thought of her as a bitch. We were still friends but I had a new best friend who didn't put on such airs.

As evidence of Suzanne's physical transformation, Julie points out Suzanne's feathered hair and tight clothes, yet Julie dressed much like Suzanne did. She too trained her hair into brittle waves and squeezed her stomach into tight jeans. The difference between them was subtle, maybe purely imaginary. Maybe they were still balloon sisters on some level, but they had turned into hallway enemies. Talking about it so many years after the fact, Julie isn't sure if Suzanne changed or only her perception of Suzanne did.

This is the way the slut rumor and the fickleness of memory work together: the rumor transforms the way a particular girl is perceived, even by kids she has known since childhood. No matter how long they have known her, the rumor becomes the dominant memory everyone has of her. Julie and her friends will now always look at Suzanne as the force five girl. Simply by being there, by being present, Suzanne evokes force five. Everything about her is permeated with it; everything about her becomes "scary and slinky."

Julie knew the boys who claimed to have participated in force five and bragged about it, but she didn't blame them. She didn't question the story or investigate it; instead, she treated the force five rumor with a kind of inevitability. One girl was bound to do it in every school, bound to disappear into the train job. It was predetermined.

To this day, Julie feels confused when she talks about Suzanne and the way this cruelty and gullibility came so easily. As she did in high school, Suzanne still has a disorienting effect on Julie. When Julie looks at the memory of Suzanne, she wonders how the war against this girl escalated so quickly, until it seemed there was no turning back. As a self-proclaimed feminist with shelves of progressive classics of the seventies and books on postmodern feminist theory, Julie thinks of herself as a forward-thinking woman. But the slut story seems so backward, and she knows she participated in it almost intuitively. She feels troubled by the way she whole-heartedly bought the force five story, how she became so caught up in it, how she experienced no trace of either suspicion or forgiveness. "I feel really weird and bad when I think about how we treated Suzanne," she says. "I feel like an idiot."

The girl Julie was in high school fades into the feverish past; when Julie reconsiders the part she played in the pageant of ostracism, she almost feels like she's looking at another person, not herself. In this way, Julie experiences a kind of cognitive dissonance—an inability to reconcile the "idiot" she was back then with the grown woman she has become.

Earlier I wrote about fear of teenagers—how they seem to disrupt the adult world by their very presence. Along the same lines, the memory of the chaotic, vengeful teenage girl threatens the grown woman who has tried to get her priorities straight, who has tried to lead a forward-thinking life. From my conversations, it was clear that when older women stared into the memory of the high school slut, they often felt like they were regressing into a better-off-left-behind aspect of female experience.

The slut wars are a gender memory that many women I talked to still could not quite reckon with. Twenty-two-year-old Amy, who spread rumors in high school, told me, "I can't believe we acted like we acted and said those things. It's amazing to me." Her amazement is the reaction of the tolerant adult looking back at the intolerant teenage self; it's similar to the way Julie felt like an idiot when she looked back at her treatment of Suzanne. The bewilderment these women felt illustrates how the girl-on-girl hatred and violence that characterize the slut phenomenon are a buried experience for many women; to speak of it is to speak of something that seems like it shouldn't have happened. They look back at themselves then, and it almost seems like they were possessed.

The distress or amazement women felt when remembering their role in ostracizing the slut can be explained, in part, as the trouble with any story that represents women negatively, not merely as victims of sexual violence or oppression but as perpetrators, as instigators. It is not a story one can learn from in any direct way, because it's so irrational—it's not a story with a moral. Particularly since the 1970s, mainstream feminist thinkers and activists have urged the production of positive role models for women. There has been the implicit understanding that women are better off telling positive stories rather than negative ones, that representing women negatively upholds a certain status quo. This belief can be found explicitly in the literature of National Women's History Month, a project with roots in the Second Wave feminist movement of the seventies. Their literature insists, among other things, that "knowledge of women's strengths and contributions builds respect and nourishes self-esteem." Through inspiration by positive role models, girls might grow up to "create a more fair and just society for all."

The hopeful elements of the positive role model story are not present in the slut story; indeed, the plot elements of the slut story speak to the ways in which girls are intuitively destructive, effortlessly imagining one another as enemies. Does this mean it is a story that should not be told? The resistance to the slut story among feminist-minded adult women I interviewed is an indication of how difficult it becomes to look back at your own negative history when the hegemonic agenda has been to look back for signs of positivity and light.

In her essential 1985 book, *Sexual/Textual Politics*, critic Toril Moi examined the work of various feminist literary critics and critiqued their work for traces of entrenched ideologies and agendas. In a chapter analyzing "images of women" criticism—which often takes authors to task for portraying women in a negative light—Moi talks about the particular Western feminist tendency to look at literature and storytelling as a prescriptive act. In analyses of groundbreaking critics like Elaine Showalter, Sandra Gilbert, and Susan Gubar, Moi questions the widespread belief that the woman reader should ideally be exposed to "strong, impressive female characters." In pursuit of impressive women who project a "seamlessly unified self," Moi argues, feminist critics often overlook texts that do not serve their purposes. There is "the assumption that good feminist fiction would present truthful images of strong women with which the reader may identify." Moi sees the tendency to always search for the whole, good, authentic woman in literature as misguided; she argues that the fragmented, bad, or inauthentic female character can tell us as much about the lives of women under patriarchy as her counterpart.

The slut story does not contain a heroine, a selfless fighter for good. It does not reflect us back to ourselves in a flattering way. It is, rather, full of lies and innuendos, and the light of meaning and truth is intermittent at best; it's a story from which no girl emerges angelic or unscathed.

Lucy, twenty-two, grew up in the South. In a phone interview she told me about how a gang of girls came after her and assaulted her one afternoon.

"This girl told me she wanted to meet me out front of school. She was a real big-haired gal. An eighth-grader. And I was like, no, I don't want to meet you out front. There was a parking lot across the street where we'd smoke. And that's where they wanted to meet. But I waited by the side of the school for my ride home. Still the girl, Hope, came and started pounding on me. She just started pounding away." Later Lucy describes walking home with a bloody nose and being afraid of school the next day for fear that Hope would come after her again.

The violence of the slut story is the violence of a cat-fight—girls threaten to scratch one another's eyes out, and through their actions they grow blind to one another. It's a violence that raises perennial questions about whether or not women would go to war if they ran the world. In 1970 Gloria Steinem wrote, "Women are sisters; they have many of the same problems, and they communicate with each other." What Steinem and many of her peers in the Second Wave feminist movement preached was that women were innately, intuitively opposed to war. At the height of the Vietnam era, the women's liberation movement and the antiwar movement were cross-pollinating, forming hybrid ideologies. The idea that grew from this period and gained ascendancy in popular media representations of feminism and "women's lib"—the versions of the feminist zeitgeist I saw on TV as a girl—was that women were natural pacifists. If women had been running the world, the argument went, the war would never have happened. In Steinem's formulation, women "communicate," while men "subjugate."

The woman who communicates instead of subjugating is an appealing idol; she carries the promise of moral superiority for the women who believe in her. It was a myth I found very appealing in my late teens and early twenties as a conscientious student taking women's history classes. ANOTHER WOMAN FOR PEACE, read my bumper sticker in college, on a red car with no headlights that sometimes poured smoke from the steering wheel. In class I memorized all the plotlines of the good feminist fight. Sometimes, especially during lectures by older women who had been on the front lines, I had the distinct sense that I had been born at the wrong time, that I should have been around back in the moment when all the rights were won. It sounded like a time of great drama and unassailable truths. It seemed like a much less ambiguous time, free of inertia or doubt.

I tried to believe in an unconditionally loving female of the species, and I blamed a lot of the problems of the world on men. I romanticized women. I consumed the propaganda of Women's History Month hungrily, and I nailed a calendar of women writers above my desk: Alice Walker, Margaret Atwood—in the photographs they had all been airbrushed to look like saints. Part of the reason hippie-era notions of women and peace appealed to me was that they promised things like "sisterhood" and a "collective"—ideal communities free of power struggles or loneliness. I wanted to be part of something big and ultimately redemptive. I wanted to believe females could save the world.

Out of college, I took a minimum-wage job at a feminist press, a struggling, cold place that encouraged submissions of stories that "speak positively to the experience of being female." It was not a happy or peaceful place to work. Among the women of the all-female staff, power struggles flourished unchecked. My boss, who looked like a sweet earth mother, was petty and cruel, full of mixed messages and little jabs. After work I'd cry into my drinks. The feminist press was such a rotten experience that it made me stop romanticizing women for good.

I had been hoping to dissolve into a collective in the same way one hopes for acceptance at the crowded table in the cafeteria, and I had formulated a vague vision of feminism out of this desire to belong somewhere. But the movement eluded me.

The vision of a tribe of peaceful women who will soothe and straighten out and redeem the world denies the vengeful violence of teenage girls and neutralizes their notorious rage. It is a vision of an angel that counteracts a monster: the monstrous female we do not want to be, the female we might remember being but are shocked by, who has the capacity to track down another girl in a parking lot and overwhelm her with all the gusto of a true predator.

What does the state of the slut tell us about the state of womankind? The slut's generalized feminist potential was explored by popular author Naomi Wolf in her 1997 book, *Promiscuities* (another book, *Slut! Growing Up Female with a Bad Reputation,* also explored the topic a couple of years later). A mixture of memoir and reporting, Wolf's book centers on stories of herself and her girlfriends coming of age. She explores her own inner struggle with the notion of being a "bad girl," concluding, "We are all bad girls, in the best possible way." Wolf argues that the shameful feelings surrounding female desire need to be relieved because they are compromising our pleasure; if the cloud of shame was lifted, the "inner slut" would introduce us to new horizons of desire.

Wolf's theory of all women having an inner slut relied on the notion that all women are essentially the same. Her book was aimed at women as a "we." Modern in its embrace of this taboo subject, Wolf's book was also old-fashioned in that she based her argument on the dream of sisterhood. In her version of this dream, we could all come to understand one another regarding the idea of the slut. We were all on the same side.

Wolf's vision of women as a broad, like-minded "we" didn't reflect the experiences of the girls I interviewed, who interpreted their existence as part of the female gender not in terms of we but in terms of us and them. As one twenty-one-year-old phrased it, "Girls are my worst enemies." And while Wolf introduced the notion of an inner slut, for the girls I interviewed there was no inner and outer; the slut story was not something they could keep inside—it was coming at them at all times from *outside.* In this state, all semblance of privacy or subjectivity has dissolved, all secrets have vanished. While Wolf argued that a girl needs to get beyond the slut in her own mind, she often blurred the boundaries between what girls imagined themselves to be and what everyone else imagined them to be.

The collective of girls who have an inner slut is one version of the story of women. Another version is this: the collective that has become a mob, in which some girls are sluts and others aren't. They are diametrically opposed worldviews. They are two sides of a looking glass.

The notion that a mob or riot mentality might be a truer reflection of the experience of being female informed a short-lived but remarkable American feminist movement in the early nineties called Riot Grrrl. Founded in the punk rock underground scenes of Olympia, Washington, and Washington, D.C., Riot Grrrl consisted mostly of female musicians who had become restless in a male-dominated scene where progressive and radical ideas were spouted while all the rituals and rules of patriarchy were continuously reenacted. Boys owned most record labels, fronted all the big bands, and dominated parties even as punk rockers proclaimed themselves revolutionaries and subversives.

Groups of girls came together and started to talk about the irony of an outsider scene where they still felt like outsiders—they decided to reinvent the underground in their own image. They put on shows, published fanzines, took over band nights at venues that had always been dominated by men. The most infamous girl of the early scene was arguably singer Kathleen Hanna of the band Bikini Kill—an enraged genius with a Valley Girl accent. In performance she often dressed like a schoolgirl and scrawled words and messages across her body; the word SLUT could often be found written somewhere on her skin.

Riot Grrrl had its roots in a scene that had always revered the revolutionary potential of teenagers. Language about a teenage underground as a force for societal change was prevalent; Sonic Youth sang about teenage riots, and record label owner and scenester Calvin Johnson proclaimed punk rock's mission was "exploding the teenage underground into passionate revolt against the corporate ogre."

Riot Grrrl co-opted the punk rock vision of teenage revolutionaries and made those revolutionaries specifically female. Although most of the girls who took part in Riot Grrrl were college age or older, they were partaking in a movement that revered the teenage girl as the ultimate prophetess or witness. They saw the adolescent standing on the edge of society, at the threshold of the paternal home, and calling into question all its beliefs. This society was called variously "bullshit Christian capitalist," "patriarchy," or "boy punk."

Riot Grrrl distinguished itself from other movements with its embrace of a kind of angry radicalism that had not been seen among white feminists in any organized fashion since the margins of the early seventies. Yet if in the seventies the issues were war and reproductive rights, for Riot Grrrl the issues were more about imaginative territory, about vague notions of creative freedom. Perhaps most of all the fight was about language, about names.

In an undated, unsigned flyer/collage called *What Is Riot Grrrl*, the one-word question "SLUT?" appears in black letters across the bottom of the page, and next to it in smaller print: "Why are people afraid that a girl would 'like' sex? Why is it anyone's business who a girl sleeps with anyways?"

In the space beneath "SLUT?" these feminist activists found an archaeological site where they might try to excavate a civilization of fears. Their flyers looked like notes passed in high school, and in performance they screamed like tantrum-throwing banshees from homemade stages. In the seventies, the cry was, "I am woman, hear me roar"; now the girls roared out in frustrated, concentrated punk rock screeches. It was exhilarating and exhausting to listen to. In "Alien She" Kathleen Hanna declares, "Feminist! Dyke! Whore! I'm so pretty ALIEN / She wants me to go to the mall / SHE wants me to put the pretty, pretty lipstick on." Watching her onstage, her face shiny with sweat and the room surging forward in delirious idol worship, the audience momentarily felt like part of something. Not a movement, exactly, but *something*.

*   *   *

Naomi Wolf's *Promiscuities* and Riot Grrrl both were part of a wider trend in the nineties of repossessing the word "slut"; by 2001, a chain store called Claire's Accessories was selling SLUT patches to high school girls, perfect for sewing on jeans or backpacks. "Slut" was no longer a word uttered only in whispers, and it seemed like in an age of irony it was losing some of its gravity, being hollowed out through repetition and various modern interrogations. Just as kids know the formulas to horror movies by heart, girls were beginning to understand the manipulative plotlines of the slut story. The girl sewing a SLUT patch on her backpack was akin to the gay man wearing a baseball hat with the word QUEER emblazoned on it—it was a form of defusing derogatory terms of their power by embracing them.

Yet the fact that the taboos have fallen down around certain words and the words can be spoken freely does not mean the words lose their history. And it doesn't mean the words lose the currency of a curse among masses of kids who enter the doors of high school every day, waiting for the slut to manifest herself. Irony goes only so far in undermining a powerful archetype.

Christine Young is fourteen years old and attends a suburban school in northern California where most of the kids are from affluent families. When I talk to her on the phone, she tells me she has been the slut of her high school for about six months. Her experience so far has been of whispers, writing on walls, guys and girls coming up to her in the hall and telling her that they heard what she had done at a party she hadn't even attended. Christine stands out physically from her classmates; she's tall and rangy, with bleached blond hair and short plaid skirts. She carries a briefcase instead of the regulation backpack. Her difference turns her into a target.

Even at fourteen, Christine is already a denizen of the punk rock and ska scenes in San Francisco. She takes trips into the city whenever there are all-ages shows and she thinks of herself as "mostly a mod, a rude girl." Christine feels that the music scene and the rock shows save her from the "totally backward" kids at school, who believe that just because she dyes her hair this color she also gives blow jobs for cigarettes. She talks about these kids as "totally sheltered and dumb," but even though she feels above them, more informed and cooler, she still has to go to school with them every day. No matter how much she has heard about the irony of the slut story, the kids around her are decidedly unironic.

Christine knows about Kathleen Hanna, about how all these cool girls on the fringes have been interrogating the whole idea of slut, writing it on their bodies, yelling about it, exposing it as a patriarchal cliché. But regardless of what she knows, she can't change the minds of the kids around her, who still believe in the cliché like a kind of gospel. Christine can't easily rise above the hormonal hallucinations that infect and invade her life at school. Sometimes when she's out in the city listening to music, she has moments when she forgets all about it, but these moments never last long enough. To rise above the experience of being the slut, to repossess or embrace it, this was an ability I found only in older girls, in their twenties and thirties. High-school-age girls were less adept at analyzing what was happening to them—in their youthfulness they had a hard time seeing past the present moment.

Maybe only after girls have finished with the wars in the hallways do they gain any perspective on why the wars came about. Christine wanted to have some distance from being the slut of the school, but no matter how many times she found a ride into San Francisco, she always had to come back home, go to school the next day, and head for her locker, where anything could await her: a red word painted across the door, a threatening note slipped through the cracks.

At the end of our phone conversation, Christine tells me, "When I saw your ad I thought, I should probably talk to this lady and see if I can give her any input. I think everyone should try and get into the whole unity thing and supporting each other. If all the girls are calling one girl a slut, unity's never going to happen."

The desire for some "unity thing" among girls that eludes them in the boy-crazy wars of the hallway is a vital and important desire; it's a theme I found recurring in my interviews as we discussed the role girls played in ostracizing the slut. It's a desire akin to my aforementioned longing for a sisterhood, and its persistence illustrates that, almost despite ourselves, we wait for some unified and new reality to show itself, some version of utopia. Girls and women who described this desire to me seemed to be saying, Maybe things don't have to be this way, maybe there is another story, another plot altogether that hasn't been explored.

Twenty-five-year-old Madeline signed her letters "Goddess Bless." She was one of a series of women who expressed sympathy or allegiance with goddess feminism. Chynna, twenty-six, said, "I am really getting into witch and goddess stuff, and I have been learning about that world." Another woman talked about being healed through believing in the goddess. These alternative forms of feminist thought locate the strength of women in a deep and buried past that existed outside of or before the era of patriarchy.

A seminal book of the goddess movement is Riane Eisler's 1988 study, *The Chalice and the Blade,* in which the author outlines evidence of a prehistoric age when women were revered as keepers of life and knowledge. Analyzing the cultural traces left behind by Paleolithic and Neolithic eras, as well as the civilizations of Old Europe and Minoan Crete, Eisler posits the existence of goddess-centered societies. In this past world, she argues, respect for the land prevailed. Female rulers were benevolent life givers, and women were "powerful and honored rather than dominated and despised." Examining the imagery of goddess-centered art, she writes: "If the central religious image was of a woman giving birth and not, as in our time, a man dying on a cross, it would not be unreasonable to infer that life and the love of life—rather than death and the fear of death—were dominant in society as well as art."

The values of the period of *The Chalice and the Blade* are presented by Eisler in opposition to the violent patriarchy that came later. Eisler sees violence and imperialism as degenerate strains in humankind, ways of straying from the soul. Eisler believes in Jesus' "original gospel of love" and writes about Christ as an original feminist—freely associating with women, befriending a whore, Mary Magdalene, and keeping her as a close confidante in his final hours before the torture that sent him to heaven and freed him of the torturing world.

It's easy to see why the goddess story might appeal to a girl like Madeline, who had spoken to me previously about a peaceful time before her slut years, when she was "happy and rode horses." Like Karen Lehman from Andover Heights, who spoke of a "beautiful pure childhood," Madeline had a tendency to look far back into the past in search of a version of the world different from the one she found herself stranded in, a world before these stifling sexual archetypes took over and closed her off from a million possibilities.

Maybe if the girl who is deemed the slut goes back far enough, she could get to a moment before all the whispers and lies, before she felt like such a freak and a loser. Maybe she could get to a point when the whore was at the right hand of God's Son, when the things written on the bathroom wall were hieroglyphs, praising her fabulous powers. Maybe if she looks far back enough, way back into prehistory, she might locate a place where a girl like her could've been ruler of the world.

8

BASEMENT HISTORIES

"Let's call this our little secret." This is the classic command given to kids who are sexually abused by adults. Many girls I interviewed testified to memories of sexual abuse by fathers or uncles or baby-sitters: some adult male with a grim and overpowering urge came toward them when no one else was around. Afterward he would inevitably give the our-little-secret speech. The commandment not to tell was obeyed for a while, often all the way through childhood and adolescence. But then the commandment wore off and girls were compelled to bear witness to the past, to recount it to therapists, friends, lovers—even a stranger like me.

Lucy wrote an e-mail letter about her uncle, who would drop by in the dead hours of the afternoon, sit her on his lap, and pull off her underwear. "He was my aunt's husband, an uncle by marriage. He was the only man in my small universe—all my other family members and teachers were women. This uncle talked to me, listened to me, spent time with me, asked me about my schoolwork. He also molested me. I thought it was my duty to allow him." For Lucy, these episodes with her uncle created the groundwork for what came later: a sexual life that she considers a nightmare, where everything seemed off-kilter and out of control.

In a phone interview, Laura told me about a baby-sitter who molested her repeatedly when she was ten. "After that it took me a while to treat sexual advances with normalcy. I felt somewhat obligated to anyone who was interested in me." Although she never had intercourse with boys, at thirteen and fourteen Laura was more sexually active than the girls in her class. She locates the beginning of her panicky habit of "putting out" in the empty hour of that baby-sitter, who had her to himself while her parents were out.

Sara was pulled into a closet once by an eighteen-year-old cousin when she was six. "He whipped his dick out and made me touch it. I told my mom about it, and she asked me what I had done to deserve it." Sara told me, "I have had a really horrific life."

Whether they had been molested repeatedly or only once, whether it was a relative or simply a friend of the family's, these girls all identified childhood sexual abuse as the beginning of a pattern of objectification, even the beginning of a "horrific life." This was where it all started, where the first traps were set. If they had somehow been able to escape from their childhood, if they hadn't been vulnerable to that first invasion, they speculated that maybe they would've never been chosen as the slut. Childhood sexual abuse and the high school slut myth were in some causal relationship, intertwined elements of the same bad destiny.

In my interviews, the girls who talked about sexual abuse far outnumbered the girls who didn't. Eventually, I realized it was an integral element of the slut story. Like precocious puberty, a suburban environment of boredom and impatience, a tendency toward extroversion, and the train job rumor, childhood sexual abuse was a constant that repeatedly played itself out in the narrative.

Twenty-eight-year-old Sharon Brown was the focus of the rumor mill; the main story about her was "the whole soccer team." When Sharon tells me her story we're in the same conference room where I interviewed Madeline, in the newspaper offices. The air is hot and our throats are dry. Sharon is wearing a T-shirt advertising the name of a sports team. She's wearing thick, Coke-bottle glasses, an opulent engagement ring. Her cheeks are flushed, as if the act of telling makes her blood rush to the surface.

Tracing backward before high school, Sharon talks about how she grew up in what she calls a "weird house." Her mom died of cancer when Sharon was six. Her dad, a laid-back hippie, invited a series of male friends to live in the too-empty house. One guy lived there for a long time. He paid too much attention to Sharon, treating her "like I was his girl-friend. I was only ten but I looked like I was sixteen. And we would make out, and eventually we started having sex."

When she was later singled out as the slut of her school, Sharon believed she was ostracized because she'd been having sex at ten years old. The motherless house where she spent all her time with men translated into the halls of school, where she was "only friends with guys." She talks about home as a place where she saw things she shouldn't have seen and was exposed to experiences she wasn't ready for. "I didn't know how to process that stuff. It made me feel really out of control." She felt that the kids could read in her eyes the secret of what she and her father's friend had been doing, as if it were written on her skin. She felt like the secret glowed at the base of her identity.

When Sharon talks about life after her mom died she describes herself as the only girl in a world of men and their desires, in which she couldn't hide behind her mom's skirts anymore. What she craved was unconditional love, but a child in Sharon's position quickly learns that love has a series of conditions attached to it—she needs to be ready at all times; she can't protest or assert her power, because she has none, even when she finds herself on the receiving end of threats, stares, touches, 3 A.M. trespasses. She can't say anything about it because no one will believe her, or at least this is what she has been told. She has also been warned that the secret would tear the house apart, and in that case, where would she live? Under the influence of these age-old manipulations, Sharon kept the secret until she was in her late teens, when the secret started to get the best of her and she found a therapist in the phone book.

*　　*　　*

In *The Common Secret: Sexual Abuse of Children and Adolescents,* psychiatrists Ruth and Henry Kempe write about patterns they've found interviewing females who'd been sexually abused. "A very young girl is trained to be a sexual object, giving and receiving sexual pleasure in order to win approval," they write. The Kempes describe the way a girl who is treated as a sexual being in childhood often develops a distorted view of the centrality of the sexual drama—she begins to feel like sexual behavior is the only true form of communication, the only true transfer of love. Their theories are supported by many researchers on the topic of childhood sexual abuse. The American Academy of Child and Adolescent Psychiatry advised in 1998: "When sexual abuse has occurred, a child can develop a variety of distressing feelings, thoughts and behaviors," including "unusual interest in or avoidance of all things of a sexual nature" and "seductiveness." Among women survivors the Kempes found "character disorders with promiscuity." Roughly translated, this means girls who told stories of being sluts.

In my interviews sometimes childhood sexual abuse stories were full of graphic details. Tricia told me about her older brother's friends, who chased her up trees, and how she had "learned to wash the cum out of [her] hair" at an early age. Other stories weren't graphic but vague, made up of hints instead of specifics. "I know I was sexually abused as a child," one girl told me. "I just can't remember who it was. I think it was my dad, but he's dead now so I can't ask him."

The details a girl gave me depended on her particular method of storytelling, the conditions of our conversation, the hour and the exhaustion level, maybe the alcohol level, maybe hormones. The intersection of the childhood sexual abuse story and the slut story occurred at a cultural moment when both stories were gaining wider and wider acceptance. Just as the taboo around the word "slut" had started to crumble, so too the story of childhood sexual abuse had emerged with a vengeance in the eighties and nineties; it had come to be understood as one of the great untold stories of women's lives. When I began conducting my interviews, the notion of a child sexualized and exploited by adults was no longer in the closet; in fact, incest confessions had become something of a cottage industry.

In the eighties and nineties the childhood sexual abuse industry took shape in books, movies of the week, and revelations by famous women like Oprah and Roseanne. The unburying of the violated inner child proved an irresistible and powerful topic, mostly for women, and it multiplied and unfolded rapidly throughout mainstream media. The most remarkable novel to hit the best-seller lists as part of this pattern of revelation was Dorothy Allison's *Bastard Out of Carolina,* although there were a myriad of others, and a myriad of *Bastard* knockoffs.

By the time I was enrolled in a writing workshop in the mid-nineties, the rule was "No incest stories, please!" My teacher had grown tired of stories built around the father's shadow crossing the bedroom door, the naive girl being preyed on, constant allusions to the underside of the Daddy's-little-girl story. Her impatience with incest literature arose in part from the fact that these stories were so invested in an image of helplessness—presenting women as passive little girls cast adrift in a cruel world. To center literature on the experience requires that the main female character never do anything, never show any agency—things are only done to her.

Feminist critics, most notably Princeton professor Elaine Showalter, honed in on this problematic aspect of the childhood sexual abuse story. They pointed out the way it seemed to encourage a culture of victimhood and infantilization. Once more the spectacle of the helpless female, without power or recourse, had gained ascendancy, just like in the horror movies I discussed earlier. For women who had been on the front lines in the sixties and seventies working to pass the ERA and legalize abortion, the idea of trying to change your childhood by talking about it endlessly seemed misguided—a waste of valuable energy that could be channeled toward political causes.

As stories of childhood sexual abuse grew more common, hysterical offshoots of the essential story appeared, most infamously claims of satanic ritual abuse or evil day-care centers where children were made to submit to bizarre forms of sexual torture. Like the rumors about the slut, the rumors of childhood sexual abuse became unhinged, graphic, and extreme as they flourished in a restless culture.

Virtually all claims of satanic ritual abuse and evil day-care centers were eventually discredited, as witnesses recanted testimonies and suggestive, coercive interviewing techniques were exposed. What believers in these phenomena seemed to ignore was the imaginative powers of children. There was a rhetoric during the whole proceeding that children wouldn't lie and make up such things. Of course, anyone who has been around children and listened to them knows that they have a knack for coming up with the most bizarre scenarios of all, and the most terrifying monsters.

In her book *Hystories: Hysterical Epidemics and Modern Media*, Elaine Showalter deconstructs the cultural hysteria that led to the emergence of phenomena like satanic ritual abuse scares. In a cursory survey, Showalter also takes on chronic fatigue syndrome, environmental illness, and Gulf War syndrome, pointing out that none of these sicknesses can be medically proven. She paints a portrait of a society unmoored by rumors and superstition, in the grip of an irrational belief that something is wrong. Showalter argues persuasively that these feelings of something being wrong are actually masked feelings of powerlessness in a less and less representative democracy. She sees the trend in childhood sexual abuse confessions as a thwarted form of feminism in which women express a deep suspicion of society but make the accusation personal instead of political.

In a chapter entitled "Recovered Memory," Showalter discusses the therapy culture that helps patients recover buried memories of childhood sexual abuse. Showalter describes her doubts about the imbalanced therapist-patient relationship, which relies on the therapist uncovering some traumatic event the patient cannot remember. She questions the high rates of sexual abuse encouraged by recovered memory therapists but is, nevertheless, reflexively apologetic about her doubts: "I have come to doubt the validity of therapeutically recovered memories of sexual abuse, but I do not wish to belittle those who believe in their memories. People do not generate these confabulations out of an intention to deceive. They may need to define an identity, to work out

anger toward the accused, or to respond to cultural pres-
sures." Asking, "Why would anyone choose to take on the
pain and turmoil of being a survivor" unless she had to,
Showalter posits, "There are many plausible answers to this
question. Some of them come from the structure of therapy
itself, from a combination of suggestibility and social coer-
cion. Some of them come from the availability of this expla-
nation for a variety of anxieties and discontents in women's
lives."

The incest story swept American culture much the way a
rumor sweeps through a high school hallway. The ensuing
discrediting of the recovered memory movement and of sky-
rocketing incest statistics in general was a necessary way of
bringing the story under some control. Books like Showalter's were the administrator saying, "All right, all right, that's
enough."

Yet like the admonishing words of administrators, Showalter's sober comeuppance didn't affect any of the girls I talked
to, who were utterly compelled to speak of childhood sexual
abuse memories. Despite the fact that such memories are
met with greater and greater skepticism, for these girls, the
memories held the key. These memories were the Genesis
story. They were memories that caused all the outlines of the
future to shift, and even now, years later, they had the power
to quicken the pulse of a girl like Sharon Brown, whose face
reddened further as she remembered her father's house.

One of Showalter's most compelling arguments in the
seamlessly persuasive *Hystories* is that by indulging in tell-all
sessions about childhood sexual abuse, women are locating
the restlessness of their oppression in a psychological realm,

confining what could be a world-changing rage to the room with a doctor's chair. I thought about Showalter's point frequently during my interviews, particularly when girls talked about how this felt like "free therapy" or told me some version of *I have only told these things to my therapist.*

Showalter argued that what happens in this kind of one-on-one interaction is a kind of reduction, a diminishing. But is it? Is the conversation in which the power of "our little secret" is overturned any less political than a letter-writing campaign or a march on Washington? I had entered these exchanges with a certain cynicism: *Oh yeah, everyone has a sexual abuse story.* This was the voice in the back of my head, the tired thought at the end of an overstimulated day. But interviewing these girls, I could not stay cynical for long—I was far too moved by them to question the veracity of their stories. I was far too overwhelmed by the trespasses they recounted. I was stunned and immobilized by the world they described, where from day one they had been in the eye of a sexual storm. I was not about to ask, "Are you sure that happened?"

The girls I interviewed felt that such abuse was the event that cut their lives in two. It was a moment of trespass that many believed had turned them into freaks; in the aftermath, they wondered how they might ever escape this destiny and get back to normal. If a girl was part of a shameful, abnormal sexual pageant in the past, does this mean she will never be normal about sex, never be like other people? Both the childhood sexual abuse story and the slut story revolve around the realization that a powerful sexual unconsciousness has possessed the people surrounding you, glazing their eyes over. They are stories about being on the other side of a projection, of being unable to stop the people around you, who seem determined to do what they do, to say what they say, to erect their civilization of secrets no matter what the cost.

People who've experienced childhood sexual abuse often express guilt about the feeling of pleasure that overcame them at the time, as if to feel anything other than an overwhelming *no* was to have somehow allowed the trespass to occur. Feeling pleasure is another version of "asking for it." Yet, of course, for a child being made famous by the eyes of the adult, there is a certain pleasure and agreeable sensation; the our-little-secret commandment can carry within it a thrilling sense of being chosen. As Lucy described it, "This uncle listened to me, spent time with me, asked me about my schoolwork." These seemed like sweet concerns expressed in tipsy visits and beer breath, proclamations of care in an overarching emptiness.

Whether girls had slept with one or a hundred men, the ones who had been sexually abused as children felt promiscuous from a very early time. As one girl explained, "I wasn't a virgin anymore after seven years old. And that thing had been taken from me, so what did I have left to lose?" Sharon Brown talked about how the kids could just sense the weird house she had grown up in. While her peers were talking about getting to first and second base, Sharon had been to fourth base more times than she could count.

Under the illusion that they had already been deflowered, these girls easily alternated between the things the kids were saying about them and the things they knew in the backs of their minds were true. Essentially the kids were saying, This girl has no boundaries. And remembering the adult crossing over her boundaries so effortlessly, the girl had to reason: Maybe they're right.

During the time she was in high school, Sharon did not have sex with many boys. But because of the head trip of living at home and being her dad's friend's de facto girlfriend, she felt like she was moving ahead of the other girls, as if she was already propelled toward adulthood by the older guy's touch. In this way, Sharon perceived herself to be a fast girl before the rumors started; she perceived herself to be totally isolated and living in a different time zone. Although there were probably many girls in her school undergoing sexual abuse at home, Sharon felt like the only one.

Thus, even if the content of the slut story in itself wasn't true, for women who had been sexualized and sexually trespassed on as children, the form seemed to fit. They felt a kind of recognition and resignation when they were called slut, and they didn't protest too much. From the beginning, they had been treated like they were asking for it. The kids who spread the rumors were only acting like everyone had been acting for a long time.

In the classic incest story of a father abusing a daughter, the father warns the daughter: *If your mother found out, I would have to leave.* Fear of the father leaving compels the daughter to keep the secret. As she grows older, she might realize that the father has never been here in the first place; she might even stop fearing the idea of his leaving, because she wants to be free of him.

Carrie, forty, recounts the sexual abuse by her father all through childhood—how he would come into her bedroom at night, sometimes peeing into the corner before he masturbated on her. She thinks this was between the ages of five and thirteen. "The thing of it was," she says, "once I became a teenager, he was totally repulsed by me. He only liked me when I was a helpless kid." Adults who prey on minors sexually usually have a very specific age preference. And the preference is almost always for children who have not passed a particular threshold of sexual self-consciousness and agency.

The child promises to keep "our little secret," but as the child becomes a teenager, surly and questioning, the lock loosens on the secret. Thus the societal fear of teenagers is rooted not only in what trouble they will get into with their new driver's licenses and raging hormones; it's a fear of what they've seen as children. It's a fear of reckoning. As they transition into maturity, as their self-awareness becomes more and more acute, teenagers reexamine the past, become suspicious of it. They see that maybe the little secrets were not so little, that maybe the secrets should be told, passed on.

Mythology warns humankind about the danger of looking back. In the Orpheus and Eurydice myth, Orpheus is ordered not to look back as he tries to lead his beloved out of the underworld. But he does look back to see if she's coming. And when he does, she is pulled into the darkness, into the underworld's oblivion. In the Old Testament, Lot and his family are ordered by God not to look back toward Sodom and Gomorrah as they leave the old world. But Lot's wife looks back and she is turned into a pillar of salt.

We fear that the past will stiffen and ruin us, that it might pull us back for good if we look too far into it. The warning from God not to look toward the ruined city is like the warning from the father in the incest story not to examine what is happening in the darkness, not to think back on the night before, when he came into her room, full of a need that eclipses her. But a girl can live only so long in the shadow of a warning; she can feel boundaryless and helpless for only so long. Then she has to make a move, to turn around, to look into the past and find a way to subvert the tyranny of its secrets.

9

RACE AND THE SLUT STORY

Twenty-three-year-old Lola lives in Los Angeles, where she works as a cocktail waitress at night. During the day, she attends Spanish and acting classes and dreams of a trip to Central America, and a small part in a Billy Crystal picture. The urban sprawl of Los Angeles is nothing like the town where she grew up, a white-hot burg off the southern part of I-5 that can be entered only by passing through barren hot hills on roads where drivers get dangerously drowsy at the wheel.

Lola's town was so small that there was only one high school. But as immigrant populations, mostly from Mexico, skyrocketed, class size increased exponentially. The school sprawled out until it was two city blocks long. Lola's graduating class consisted of over fifteen hundred students. Within this vast river of kids, there were some who considered Lola the slut. She was not the slut of the entire school, since the school was too big for that. Instead, her reputation lived on the lips of twenty or so people who went to the same parties and swore she had been doing things at parties that no girl had ever done before. Lola tried to deny the rumors, to make her classmates understand that just because she had sex with boys didn't mean she would have sex with every boy who asked.

"I had been having sex since I was thirteen," she tells me. "I had fallen in love then and had sex. After that, after we broke up, I still wanted to keep having sex with guys. But there were a lot of people who thought there was something wrong with me. My best friend was jealous and she would tell people things about me that weren't true. She would try to make me feel ashamed of myself."

Almost a decade later, Lola immediately falls into a posture of dishing dirt on this lost girlfriend, telling me how ugly she was, how she had no sex life and no fun. "Guys would not ask her out. They wouldn't even try to pick up on her." Lola floats the theory that maybe her girlfriend's sexual attitudes and hang-ups had to do with being white. While Lola's half Mexican, she describes her ex–best friend as "an uptight Wasp."

"A lot of times white girls feel ashamed about sex," Lola says. "The way they are brought up and stuff. My mom is white and my dad is Mexican. My mom knew about how uptight it gets for white girls. She tried to be open about everything. On the other hand, my white friends—their parents would say, 'Oh sure, you can talk to us about sex,' but the girls knew they couldn't because their moms would freak! I knew one white girl who when her mom found out what she was doing, she kicked her out forever."

Lola brings a question to the surface that has been simmering in the back of my mind since I began my research: Is the high school slut myth I've been tracking confined to white America? Is there a relation between a Puritan past and the overwhelming desire to tell train job stories? While in my quest to find girls who were the high school slut I canvassed broadly—taking out ads in newspapers catering to nonwhite demographics, interviewing women at the local Hispanic center, cultivating and expanding on the calls from nonwhite girls—far more white women responded to my survey than nonwhite women. Overwhelmingly, white women were the ones who wanted to talk about their high school slut days.

My interviews with white women surfaced an almost eerily similar series of conditions—early puberty, early childhood sexual abuse, a tendency toward extroversion, a rumor that will not die about doing the entire football team. And as I have discussed, very often the dramas unfolded against suburban backgrounds. When white suburbanite Karen from Andover Heights cradles her head in her hands and says, "Oh my God, don't even *talk* about the football team rumor! I heard that one *so many* times," she expresses exhaustion in the face of a seemingly endless cliché. But the story we both know too well has a boundary as surely as the neighborhood does. If slang and pop culture references do not cross the color barrier, neither do clichés. My interviews with non-white women did not yield the same moments of recognition, the same eye rolling in the face of the infernally familiar story.

When I discuss the word "slut" with an eighteen-year-old woman from Puerto Rico, she seems confused. "Well, I think what you are talking about is a puta, which is 'pig' in English; this is the way we say it." LaShawn, a twenty-two-year-old African-American woman from inner city Philadelphia, says, "No we don't use the word 'slut,' we say 'whore' or 'skank.'"

LaShawn tells me the story of her evolution as an infamous whore. The story contains many of the same ingredients from white girls' stories: her name written on bathroom walls—FOR A GOOD TIME CALL LASHAWN—flocks of boys following her around begging for blow jobs because they heard "that is what I liked to do." Yet there are ways in which LaShawn's experience is essentially different from the white girls' stories I heard. LaShawn did not, for example, experience her bad reputation as something that isolated and separated her from other girls; she didn't feel like there was no one out there who understood her. "Me and my girlfriends hung out all together in a gang. Even though a lot of people said I was a whore and I sometimes thought of myself as one, because I did sleep with quite a few guys, I always had my girlfriends. We looked out for each other." And while many white girls associated the slut experience with a feeling of vulnerability, LaShawn dismisses these feelings of powerlessness with impatience in her voice. "Nobody fucked with us. People realized we were not to be messed with."

Is the dissonance between the story LaShawn tells and the story I hear from white girls a symptom of a fundamental dissonance between black and white girls? Theorists of the "girl experience" like Dr. Mary Pipher (*Reviving Ophelia: Saving the Selves of Adolescent Girls*) have often relied on a belief that there is one story of girlhood, but more and more proof arises that this is not so. Girlhood itself, the whole idea of being the female of the species, is destabilized across race and class lines. Girlhood is a state that is rhetorically assumed to be eternal, but it's not.

When considering girlhood and its variations across cultural borders and boundaries, in particular racial boundaries, perhaps no research is more informative than the increasingly well documented discovery that black girls don't experience the eating disorder anorexia nervosa. In a paper called "Racial Difference in Women's Desires to Be Thin," published in the *International Journal of Eating Disorders*, authors Andrea D. Powell and Arnold S. Kahn write,

> Using self-reports, we found that white women chose a significantly thinner ideal body size than did Black women, and expressed more concern than Black women with weight and dieting. White women also experienced greater social pressure to be thin than did Black women. White men indicated less desire than Black men to date a woman with a heavier than ideal body size, and White men felt they were more likely to be ridiculed than did Black men if they did date a woman who was larger than the ideal.

Later the authors write, "Black culture appears to 'protect' black women from eating disorders by providing an environment in which extreme thinness is less valued."

Anorexia is overwhelmingly absent from black society because the ideal body type white girls seek is not an ideal for black girls. The cult of thinness is not a cult black girls tend to believe in; the disappearing waif is not a figure that holds any power over them. The anorexia findings, and the difference in ideals they point to, illustrate that there is no one story of girlhood, because there is no one set of ideals called the feminine.

Like the anorexic, the slut is usually a white girl. Although there have been moments in my research when I've desired a universal story that would be understood by anyone listening to it, when Puerto Rican or black girls say, "I do not know what you're talking about," or, "That is not what we say," I have to admit that this is a pipe dream. No story arrives without the shadow of its contradiction, the trace of what it erases, what it cannot encompass.

Just as the word "slut" did not translate to many girls I interviewed, so too the whole idea of *high school* is not universal or unanimous. Each high school is its own world, with its own language. Each school is a noisy distillation of the neighborhood where it is constructed, the busing policies of the city where it's situated, the ghosts of the America in which it is geographically located, and the economic conditions of the families whose kids enter the automatic doors and take their standardized tests.

One of the greatest documentarians of the divergencies in the experience of school and of growing up in America is Jonathan Kozol. An activist for public school reform since the sixties, Kozol has long worked to document what he calls "segregation still existing in a so-called democracy" within the public school system. The book that made him famous, *Death at an Early Age*, recounted his experiences as a teacher in a poor Boston neighborhood. That was during the sixties, on the cusp of the civil rights movement, and Kozol wrote about the spiritual degradation of "the Negro" with outrage.

Decades later Kozol is still writing about the children and teenagers who live in the lowest tiers of a segregated society. His 1995 book, *Amazing Grace*, described a South Bronx neighborhood where the violence was unrelenting, blunting the lives of the area's children, who often suffered from depression, asthma, and recurring dreams of death. Kozol writes, "What is it like for children to grow up here? What do they think the world has done to them? Do they believe that they are being shunned or hidden by society? If so, do they think that they deserve this? What is it that enables some of them to pray? When they pray, what do they say to God?"

If in the sixties Kozol advocated tirelessly for school reform, for equality in general, these days his outrage and idealism have been tempered by a kind of wonderment. In television interviews after the release of *Amazing Grace*, he expressed amazement that things have not changed very much since the days of Martin Luther King, that despite the gains of the civil rights movement, he mostly finds that politicians pat him on the head and tell him to run along when he comes to them with his harsh portraits of children and teenagers. In the course of his brilliant career, Kozol has moved from a posture of believing in the dream of integration to intermittently wondering if it will ever come to pass.

Kozol's dream of compassion as a force for political change was shared by Martin Luther King. King argued that what was missing from the world is compassion; if only people could cross over, out of the narrow, stifling realm of the self, they would embrace humanity. Both Kozol and King lament the rarity of compassion in a nominally civilized world. It is perhaps rarest of all in the world of the high school, which is not a compassionate place by any stretch of the imagination.

In the hallways at Calhoun, I can see that the archaic impulse to separate along lines of race, to stay away from the individual who is different, still persists. During the time I spend in the cafeteria, I notice a couple of Vietnamese boys who every day sit alone at a table in the corner of the cafeteria, speaking in their native language. It's Multicultural Week, but no one has bothered to bring them into the story. They sit there very much alone, and no one even looks at them. The white girls swish past, collecting pennies for the penny wars.

When I finally approach these boys, one named Tranh agrees to talk to me for a moment. His friend, who looks irritated, will not talk and stares at the table until Tranh finishes. When I ask Tranh about his past, he tells me about his father, who fought in Vietnam on the American side. When the war was over, their family was given carte blanche by the INS to come to America. That is how they found their way here, to this suburb where girls perform Scottish jigs in the cafeteria to celebrate their heritage.

Tranh's parents run a Vietnamese restaurant. In school, he

says, he mostly spends time by himself; he likes math alright and doesn't like any teachers in particular. He shrugs when I ask him if he feels like he fits in. "I feel small here," he says, finally. "But I don't mind that." Tranh is another reminder that there is no one form of being an outsider in high school in a racially stratified society and a country of immigrants. High school and adolescence have been romanticized as a threshold state when the rebel without a cause drives too fast. Through the image of the alienated teen, myths are perpetuated about the outsider status all kids feel. But the feeling of alienation shifts; maybe it exists not in the threshold between the kid one was and the adult one is becoming but in the threshold between one's native tongue and the language of the adopted country.

Racism found its way into the slut story; the two forms of ostracism intersected. "I kissed a black boy in a racist school, and after that, all the kids said I was a slut and a nigger lover," says twenty-eight-year-old Stephanie, a white girl who grew up in the Midwest. Twenty-three-year-old Abby was called a kike by the kids around her, "a bunch of neo-Nazi anti-Semites." For both Stephanie and Abby, the slut rumors were mixed up with racial epithets. Name-calling and taunts were often a heady mixture of racial and sexual insults, parallel hateful languages.

In the feverish minds of kids, dizzy with hormones and ignorance, the fear of the slut coincides with a fear of difference. To shout or whisper "Kike" or slip a girl a Nazi pamphlet in her locker is all part of the same attempt to banish the stranger or the unknown quantity from the story. And the banishments are equivalent: "slut," "skank," or "nigger lover"—

any of these terms will elicit a response, get under the skin. They are words kids relish because they seem more powerful than ordinary words; they're "curses" and therefore have some sort of diabolical power. As the words take shape in kids' mouths, they experience a visceral thrill of transgression, a feeling of power over the powerless object of the name, a feeling of control over someone else's blood as it rushes to their face. To cause humiliation is to exert control, and to exile another kid is to prove you belong, you are here. I WAS HERE is the cliché of high school rest room graffiti.

Dee is a twenty-four-year-old Vietnamese woman living in San Francisco. She can't forget her high school days at a small East Coast prep school. Since the kids around her were mostly white, "They called me a gook and a rice eater." Yet right beneath or simultaneous with the racial harassment, the slut story took shape. Kids spread rumors that she did it with boys in the graveyard, even though on the night in question, "I was at home watching TV. I was a virgin the whole time they were saying these things. I had big boobs, though. Plus I was Oriental. What a combo." Instead of calling her "slut," the kids told her, "Go back home on the boat."

Dee's difference threatened the kids and confused their imaginations. By telling her to "go back home on the boat" while also spreading sexual rumors about her, they seem to equate her racial mystery with sexual mystery. That her skin color points toward a world outside the boundaries of their neighborhood makes kids treat her like the proverbial girl from the other side of the tracks. "Go home on the boat" is similar to "Stay away from my boyfriend" or "Don't ever come back to school" in its admonition to banishment. All of these warnings assume that this girl needs to leave or the natural order of things will be threatened.

For Abby, Stephanie, and Dee, the sexual and racial epithets floated on the same stream, the same current of air; they appeared in the same level of voice, the same quality of whisper. Words came out of car windows and were written in every phone booth, full of velocity and violence, the voices that uttered them dripping with hatred and pleasure and strange need.

When the various curses broke the air apart, the girl had to decide whether to give words the weight of gravity, and allow them to drag her down, or to behave as if the words had no weight whatsoever. She could swirl around, react, show what she was feeling, or she could walk down the hall and stare straight ahead, scan the horizon as if looking for a sign of grace.

In an essay titled "The Future of the Race," African-American activist and writer Cornel West sets forth the idea of what he calls a "colonized mind, body, and soul." In West's vision, the black experience in America is the experience of one who has been colonized—who has had his or her ancestral and spiritual country stolen. The struggle toward selfhood and equality requires breaking out of the colony one is born into and releasing oneself from the shackles of the colonizer's world.

West vividly evokes an America in which black people live with a corrosive historical memory of their own captivity. He argues that one cannot simply "overcome" captivity, since it is a state of bondage that lives in the soul and the mind, even when the chains of physical bondage have disappeared. West's work is diametrically opposed to the logic of conservative politicians, who aim to roll back affirmative action policies by arguing that racism is behind us. West's writing is a reminder that racism is really not so far behind us but is still right outside our doors.

West divides the world into the colonizers and the colonized. The colonizers are invaders, they take prisoners, they hold whole races captive. They appear in swarms, in mobs, and they negate that which they do not understand and cannot perfectly subdue. A colonized soul lives on the other side of the mob's arbitrary whims, in a place they did not ask for and did not create, inside a power imbalance that possesses the people around them like an irresistible intuition. The colonized person lives on the receiving end of a series of projections. There's a great dissonance between the stories in the dominant culture that take the colonized as their object and the stories the colonized tell themselves.

America continually reenacts the colonial drama of racism, the irrational hunger of the mob's rule. Within the culture of American schools, the violence of history reasserts itself in the games kids play, out behind the school building, away from the eyes of adults and the influence of the "civilized" world.

One particularly nightmarish story is told by Marie, the eighteen-year-old recovering drug addict. After she tells me about how "badly I had it" she tells me about how "one girl had it a lot worse than me."

"This girl's name was Roxanne. She was half black, half white, or she looked like that. I felt bad for her because she's not popular and she's not well liked. Everyone says she is a slut, like they say about me. I mean, I don't like her very much. She's not a nice person. But she was really inhumanely treated. She was duct-taped to a tree. It's a ritual out in the woods behind the school. You find a freshman and you tape them to a tree; usually it's taped pretty loose, and you can wiggle out of it. But this time they duct-taped her head and her mouth and her eyes and they spit on her and poured ketchup on her and wrote all over her face SLUT WHORE in black permanent marker. I had a pocketknife with me and I could see that she couldn't breathe so I cut a space to breathe over her mouth, and I started untying her, and this guy was like, 'What are you fucking doing, you little slut? Untaping your lesbian lover?'"

Like a lynch mob in early America, the kids took Roxanne out into the forest. In this story, which comes to me quickly and breathlessly, Marie untapes Roxanne's mouth; after that I do not know what happened. What I do know is that both girls occupied and witnessed events in a dark wood, where violent impulses move unchecked and old mob dreams arise again and again like the images in a ghost story. But which one is stronger? The old story, the archetype? Or the girl who breaks away from the mob, takes the corners of the tape between her fingers, and helps the other girl escape?

In an essay entitled "Sisters of the Yam," black feminist theorist bell hooks writes witheringly about white feminists

Naomi Wolf and Katie Roiphe. In discussing their books *The Beauty Myth* and *The Morning After,* respectively, hooks identifies a trend in "feminist criticism by young white privileged women who strive to create a narrative of feminism . . . that denies race or class differences." Wolf and Roiphe, hooks posits, do not "test many of their assumptions to see if what they have to say about feminism and female experience is true across race and class boundaries."

Reading hooks, I have to wonder about my own white predisposition. Like Lola's girlfriend I am a Wasp, and in this Wasp state I am a colonizer, a girl of privilege, sitting in the hallway doing her extra-credit assignments. I am trying to tell a story of high school sluts but I am wary that the telling itself is a form of colonizing.

Does the fact that mostly white women answered my survey mean that this is a story that isn't worth telling? Should this story be diluted in some way, changed so that it is more inclusive and therefore more important? Eventually I realize, as I ponder hooks's words of warning, that I am not telling a story about female experience; rather, I am telling the story behind a very particular phrase that some females (and males, of course) experience with a visceral rush. Others don't.

The phrase "high school slut" evoked specific memories for me, and I think there was a point where I ended and the phrase itself took over. The phrase followed the grooves in the mind of the world, grooves that have been established through racial separation. The nonwhite girls who did not identify "high school slut" as a powerful phrase were, in essence, saying: That is not our word, that is yours. Take it.

Because high school is a tribal place, the story of the slut is in many ways informed by the irrational logic of tribalism. The girls who called me, who recognized what I was saying and leaned across the table on fire with their version of the story, were part of the same tribe I was part of. The language I was speaking was not part of a universal or inclusive memory, but rather a tribal memory only certain people responded to.

To talk about the high school slut is another way of talking about America, and just as America is a vaporous notion, always shifting, always full of new believers and new contradictions, so too the high school slut archetype dissolves at certain points, becomes almost imperceptible. Some people swear they can see her clearly, others swear she was never there at all.

10

GETTING OVER HIGH SCHOOL

Any day now, any day now, I shall be
released.

—Bob Dylan

As kids near graduation, high school counselors pass out pamphlets about "realizing your potential" and "making career choices." The pamphlets are part of the process of recruiting kids on the path to a hopeful future. They represent adulthood as a beckoning and unthreatening frontier: "A world of possibility awaits!" When seniors graduate, they walk up to a podium as the crowd applauds them for having made it, having arrived. It's called commencement—the beginning, the starting out of "real life." That the graduates are all wearing the same robes and cardboard hats has a leveling effect; it's as if they are all now part of the same pool of humanity and they can no longer be distinguished from one another.

But everyone learns the world does not really begin again once one leaves high school; in fact, the role one plays among the tribes of adolescence imprints itself indelibly on memory and comes back in dreams. High school refuses to leave, surfacing in those much-recounted nightmares of the test one didn't study for or of showing up for class naked.

High school is the period when one's identity is stripped away and reconstructed, a point of crossing over. We call it a "rite of passage": the phrase is about being tested, wondering if one will be able to make it through the crucible of adolescence. Yet for girls whose passage down the hallway was often greeted by catcalls and whispers, this rite of passage is a particular challenge; the journey is not easily forgotten and will always return when they least expect it.

Some girls I interviewed had been cast in the role of the slut for six years or more, beginning in junior high school. For these girls, the imprint of that period was like a brand, even in adulthood. Sometimes they talked as if the past was more real to them than the present, and they were sure that if they did not watch their backs the past would overtake them. They would be arrested by their old reputation, stopped in their tracks, and extradited across the boundary of time.

Ex–high school sluts now in their twenties and thirties were chemists, rabbis, strippers, cocktail waitresses, teachers, yoga experts, hairdressers to the stars, magazine writers, and housewives. They were married or three times divorced, gay or straight, alone or family-bound. Some felt they had the slut period in perspective as one era in a series of years that make up a life, while others zeroed in on that period as the catalyst for everything that happened since.

Throughout my interviews with adult women, I heard the story of the flashback: a man in a grocery store gives a grown women a *look* that propels her back to high school, or the tone of a girlfriend's voice suddenly recalls an earlier betrayal. For one girl in her late thirties, a drippy guy at a wedding reception made a stupid comment about her shirt "working hard" to cover her breasts, and this caused her to leave the party immediately in the grip of an overpowering nausea.

At commencement the speakers talk about the future as if it is safe from the past. But the past exerts its dominance over the future. A woman can be transformed back into the high school slut by a small, seemingly minor turn of events. She can be on the road to the future and find herself in a head-on collision with her old self. *Not so fast,* this old self says. *I'm still here.*

Margaret O'Brien basks in her past history, wearing the word "slut" like an advertisement. At twenty-six, she's years beyond being the Healy Park Whore in suburban Texas. When we meet, Margaret is wearing tights decorated by the word *Slut!* It's written in a white-on-black pattern, in about twenty-five-point type. An official-looking, medical-style name tag on her coat also reads *Slut*. She wears deep red lipstick and a push-up bra showing remarkable cleavage. She tells me, "I would *love* to talk about being the high school slut!"

When she was twelve, Margaret moved from San Francisco, a city of lefty liberals, to a town in Texas she describes as "rich, totally snobby, full of conservative Southern belles. They all thought I was a complete weirdo." Margaret had big breasts back then, and the kids wouldn't stop staring. A boy in her class took her out on a date, took her home, "and I realized now he raped me. We were both twelve. There weren't words like 'date rape' then. I thought rape was in an alley with a stranger jumping out at you." This boy went to school the next day and told the kids how Margaret "put out." From then on, until graduation from twelfth grade, she says, "My life was a living hell. Every Friday night a gang of boys would come around and throw rocks at my window. They were yelling, 'Come on! Come on down and blow us!' "

At this point Margaret is laughing hard, remembering the desperate boys in their ragtag gang, calling her Healy Park Whore (or HPH for short), begging for blow jobs. "I mean, *how pathetic can you get?*" she says.

Margaret says that for a while being the slut of the school "really hurt. But one day I just stopped caring. I remember the day I stopped caring, actually. I was walking down the hall and this football player asks, 'Hey, Margaret, what are you doing this weekend? I heard you gave Carl Miller a blow job last weekend and I was wondering if you would give me one.' I just looked at him. I couldn't believe it. And then I just started laughing my ass off."

When Margaret realized the absurdity of all these boys pleading for a girl they had seen in a porn movie, a girl memorialized as a "hore" because of their inability to spell, all she could think to do was laugh. She felt sorry for all of them, sorry for how powerless they were in the face of her heart-stopping cleavage. At twenty-six, she relishes her sexual power, puts herself on display: she bleaches her hair and drives a convertible and waits for the inevitable truck drivers to honk. Free of the slut period but now defining herself as a "complete slut," Margaret seems to occupy a place above and beyond her high school years, while also reveling in nostalgia for them. She is over being the slut, but she is also more the slut than ever—she has accepted it as her glorious, sex-crazed destiny.

If Margaret was the queen of positive feelings, dark-eyed Madeline from Calhoun High was an impressive fountain of negativity. She was the source of a story I call "the punch," which had a strangely inspirational effect on the girls I recounted it to.

As Madeline tells it, the night of the punch began well. She was out on the town in Seattle, at a new martini bar. "Me and my friend Meg were out with these guys from a really cool band. We were dressed to the nines, so people were looking at us and we felt totally hot. All of a sudden this girl comes up and she is being real nice, probably 'cuz she wants to get with the guys in the band, and she is like, 'You're Madeline, right? Remember me? We went to high school together.' I was drunk but then all of a sudden I remember who she was, this really popular girl who was one of the worst offenders. Telling lies about me all the time. Yelling names at me from her car when she was driving away from school."

The popular girl came up to Madeline that night in the bar offering an apology for the crimes of the past. According

to Madeline, the girl said, "I am really sorry. I think the reason we did it has something to do with how, when something
is beautiful, you want to destroy it." Madeline rolls her eyes
when she tells me that the girl went on and on, an alcohol-
fueled monologue, a confession.

Madeline didn't buy it. The forgiveness this girl was asking for seemed so puny, so late. Madeline stared at the girl for
a moment. Then she punched her in the face.

Although they seem like temperamental opposites, both
Madeline and Margaret are denizens of the Goth subculture—fans of Nine Inch Nails, Anne Rice novels, dressing in
corsets and fishnets. Other women I meet are punks, mods,
bikers. What's consistent is the tendency among these women
to embrace a subculture, to see themselves as moving beneath
the story of the normal. The counterculture lives in opposition
to the culture where the former slut was ostracized and left
out, where her name was a joke.

The archetypal home-wrecking slut is on the outside of
family life, looking in; she will never be a "perfect mother."
Girls I interviewed had internalized this sense of being outside the mainstream, and it often led to a heightened sense of
freedom, a tendency toward exploration and experimenta-
tion. Because they had been singled out as freaks from early
on, many women felt like they now had nothing to lose by
exploring the subcultures of freaks.

The promise of a counterculture is the promise that
maybe this is a realm where home can be reinvented. A thriving subculture's ability to replace, and maybe even erase, the

home and family is why people will always be forming new languages, new clubs and private bars, new fanzines that only insiders can read. Subcultural America is in some ways an extension of the tribalism of high school. Yet for girls who were the sluts of the school, who felt chosen and picked on by the tribes, embracing a subculture made them feel they were choosing their own tribe, their own fate, their own symbolic life.

Forty-one-year-old Suzannah, a masseuse who has been through years of psychotherapy since her slut days, took to the road with a biker gang after high school. "My family was really screwed up," she says, and their dysfunction only compounded the pain of being the high school slut. She had come out of adolescence wanting more than anything to find some sense of belonging. With the bikers, she says, "I could really be a freak, and it was OK. It was like a family." She credits the biker experience with her current positive outlook. "I am really happy. I think things are going to be OK from now on." Some part of the girl who could not escape, who could not get far enough away, was absorbed on the bikers' open road.

Since many women I interviewed were suburban kids who had moved to urban centers when they reached adulthood, their voyage into the city presented the possibility of being absorbed by the crowd instead of being singled out by it. The city was seen as a place where their identity could be cast off and a new self could be generated from the noise and the smog. San Francisco, Los Angeles, New York, even Newark, New Jersey—throughout our conversations the city was a shining, anonymous place where peace could be found in the fact that when people were whispering, they were whispering names and stories that had no hold over you.

Whether a girl could actually move away from her hometown depended on her economic status and her emotional resilience, and often even when she did move to the city, she found herself drawn back by family, friends, and homesickness. Old sick feelings and sadnesses would come back when, as one woman described, "you go into this bar when you are home for Christmas, and all the old motherfuckers are there, standing around looking at you. It doesn't matter what you have done with your life, they will *always* look at you like the slut!"

In *The History of Sexuality*, volume one, philosopher Michel Foucault mused on the West's obsession with sexual confession. He posited that although the common story is about how sex is "repressed" and somehow hidden from view, really the West more than any society before or since has been obsessed with creating a discourse of sex, of talking the whole phenomenon and mystery into the ground. Foucault writes:

It may well be that we talk about sex more than anything else, we set our minds to the task; we convince ourselves that we have never said enough on the subject, that, through inertia or submissiveness, we conceal from ourselves the blinding evidence, and that what is essential always eludes us, so that we must always start out once again in search of it. It is possible that where sex is concerned, the most long-winded, the most impatient of societies is our own.

Foucault wrote about what he called "this strange endeavor, to tell the truth of sex." He posited that maybe the truth would never be reached, that sex would always remain a mystery no matter how much we spoke of it. In tracing the outlines of the slut myth and talking to girls who had endured it, I had to wonder if there was any way to get to the bottom of this story, or if it would always have this irrational grip on the mind of people on both sides of it. Can you talk your way into the interior of the myth? Can its mysteries be exposed through words? This was something we were all trying to answer as we let the minutes slip by, telling one more story of the train job legend, one more story of the unbelievable crude past in thrall to the dirty mind.

Because many of the girls I interviewed came to me through the sex column "Savage Love," they were generally girls immersed in the kind of no-holds-barred sexual conversation that Dan Savage represents—a way of talking about sex that eschews conventional manners and taboos. "Savage Love" is an important element in understanding the trends in talking about sex that inform the slut story I have been tracing.

As a veteran of the ACT-UP movement in the early nineties, Dan Savage began writing his column in the midst of the AIDS culture wars. He adopted a radically open writing style that is now referred to as in-your-face. This way of talking about sex made the conversation itself seem like a confrontation. "Hey Faggot," readers addressed their early letters (a salutation Savage eventually dropped). Before Savage, sex columnists had primarily taken the voice of therapists, maternal, unthreatening women writers, or doctor figures. Savage changed the tone of the argument. There was and is throughout his columns an impatience with shame or any breed of closeted individual. He argues that "perversion" is normal and that attempts to normalize and regulate sex are based in fear of sex.

Savage's rage and impatience appealed deeply to the girls I interviewed, and many were hard-core fans. They felt like what he was doing—dragging everything out of the closet— was a necessary act. And while Savage's column was in some ways what the media business calls a crossover column, it was also a column very much for and about gay men, informed and compelled by an outrage about the sexual ostracism gay men undergo. I previously discussed how the fag and the slut have in many ways occupied the same whispering hallway. As the girls I interviewed tried to tell the truth of sex, they kept coming across scenarios that had no place in girls' magazines or in erotic coming-of-age tales like Naomi Wolf's but that fit better into the blunt talk of a gay cultural icon like Savage. Sixteen-year-old Darby, from southern California, told me, "For a long time when I looked at my past I would just see a violent porno." Writers like Savage encouraged her to stare into the violent porno, to be unafraid of describing the sexual story at the depths of imagination and memory, to pull everything possible out of the closet and into the light.

To talk about sex, to decide that there is nothing wrong with talking about it, to realize perhaps it is the most important language of one's life—this was a decision the girls I interviewed had to make in order to understand the power the slut myth had maintained over them. But they were not merely talking about sex for the thrill or the pleasure of it, or even because they wanted to be daring or hip. They talked about it because they needed to tell their side of the story. They were like seekers of justice who wanted someone, anyone, to know what they had really done, as opposed to what people said they had done.

If these girls had no qualms when it came to talking about sex, many of them complained that sex itself, the mystery of it, was lost to them. They could try to make sense of it, but they could not get lost in it. Sex was too charged with rage and bad memories to ever be a thing of pure, uninterrupted pleasure.

Many of the girls I interviewed in their twenties and thirties rarely experienced orgasm. While sexuality researchers have found this to be a widespread phenomenon among women, and while the elusive Big O is the subject of countless girl talk columns and *Cosmo* articles, for the women I interviewed the elusiveness of orgasm struck me as particularly ironic. While, in high school, they had been considered monsters of pleasure, out of control in their pursuit of sex, they were, in reality, girls for whom the great goal of sex often seemed out of reach. Some felt like they had never really gone all the way.

Tricia, twenty-two, said to me, "I have never experienced orgasm, and I've had damn good sex." She attributes her inability to have an orgasm to the fact that her sexual imagination was formed during the slut period; now when she feels vulnerable or too opened up to a guy, bad memories come flashing back. So she stops and pulls back before the moment of climax. Her observation—that the idea of letting go seemed dangerous—was echoed by a large number of girls I interviewed. Sexual pleasure was interrupted by mistrust. No matter how blissful a girl felt, she couldn't shake the feeling that something bad was about to happen.

If the pleasures of love elude you, if you come across troubling reminders and flashbacks everywhere, it is possible to fall under the spell of the death drive. When I asked how life had been after high school, many girls described a growing feeling of having no future, nowhere to go. Because in high school they'd been turned into characters in the crowd's story, once out in the world, they found it difficult to project themselves onto the screen of the future, to see themselves as anything but the shattered character from the past. So some became depressed or self-destructive. Some girls had taken to heart the notion that they were cursed.

If you believe a bad spell has been cast on you from the beginning, it becomes easy to desire the cessation of everything. For thirty-five-year-old Karen from Andover Heights, the death drive was and still is the ghost in her head, hammering her with questions like, *Why are you here? Will your life* ever *get straightened out?* She has doubts about her ability to cope. She exudes an intense fragility.

It would seem that a girl who had endured the kind of things Karen has would want to leave Andover Heights immediately. She considered it hell on earth, after all, and the aim of all the myths is to get *out* of the underworld. But

Karen explains that for a long time she couldn't summon the motivation to leave and remained there for fifteen years after high school. Eventually she moved into an apartment right at the center of town, with windows on all sides allowing everyone to see in. Just as in high school, Karen was once again on display for the whole town, in a glassed-in freak booth like a girl in quarantine.

On the street every day she'd run into people from high school and relive her humiliation in their sidelong glances. When depression completely blindsided her she'd hide out in her apartment for days, skipping work, lying beneath a drift of blankets. Once she maxed out her credit card for a trip to Hawaii, a purchase that drove her into bankruptcy. Other things she would buy when she could not afford them: lipstick, soap, expensive perfume.

Karen's most self-destructive moments happened under the influence of drugs. She has come precariously close to overdosing a few times. She became friends with a crack addict, and she remembers blanked-out nights wandering along the railroad tracks with this woman. She remembers tripping on the tracks and breaking her ankle but continuing to walk on it because the drug mission had not yet been completed.

Sometimes her car, a trashed, small vessel with bald tires, would beckon to her. Karen would strap herself inside the car late at night when she was feeling particularly down-and-out. She'd drive out to the turnpike, which ran along the border of Andover Heights. She'd get into the fast lane, floor it, accelerate to ninety miles an hour. Then she'd turn out the headlights.

"When I would really get going so fast and then just be hurtling through the darkness, I would taste the sweet taste of oblivion," Karen says.

When Karen accelerated the car, moving without lights in the fast lane, she believed, on some level, that she was daring the dark road of the merciless town to swallow her up. She couldn't believe it hadn't swallowed her already.

Although after high school the tribes disperse, becoming mostly powerless, nomadic, the visceral memory of who was popular and who was cruel can still be enough to send Madeline's fist flying into a drunken girl's face. Many girls I interviewed said that they wanted to go back to the scene of their worst nightmare and "show everybody." One woman talked about how she was contemplating wearing "only a G-string to my tenth-year reunion." Another said, "Here I am making a lot of money with my own salon." Nodding her head in amazement, she continued, "And everyone told me I was a nympho psycho." Women who were successful in their fields mused: *If only they could see me now.*

Maybe these women would never make it back to the high school reunion and show everyone, but many felt that simply by going back even in their own minds and looking at the years of being the slut, by finding a way to represent and articulate what had occurred, they were rescuing themselves from the futureless oblivion Karen adored. The women who seemed strongest, who seemed like they were going to be released from their past, had taken the slut experience and represented it, whether through painting, writing, or performing. One girl had been painting canvases of her old locker that had evil spray-painted words all over it. Another told me proudly, "I wrote a story about this, and it was published!" An actress said that she channeled the hallway girl into a dramatic role, and she felt like the role allowed her to process the events of the past.

The feminist act of bearing witness means moving backward into history and reckoning with it, not only as a way of uncovering the sources of one's neuroses or as a way of blaming a past event for all that went wrong, but as a way of actually *seeing* what happened so the disintegrated self can once again be whole. In this formulation, the girl who was once swallowed by her own life now stares into the jaws of life. But she isn't swallowed or consumed.

Adrienne Rich's poem "Diving into the Wreck" makes a permanent metaphor out of this feminist act of bearing witness. For Rich, bearing witness is like the work of a diver who must document a shipwreck in a mythic ocean. The diver moves into the sea wearing an awkward suit and heavy flippers. The sea is an area beneath understanding and consciousness; on its floor the diver finds the wreck, covered with algae. At the poem's crescendo, Rich writes about the purposes of diving—to witness all that has been lost, all that has crashed or failed, to look down into the lightless depths of a life instead of always trying to look toward the sun: "I came to explore the wreck," she writes. "I came to see the damage that was done / and the treasures that prevail."

The slut is a myth created in the ocean of unconsciousness, and the girls who wanted to retrieve her, revisit her, and reckon with her wanted to travel down into the myth's hull, its undeniable scene of damage. These girls have seen a wreck of the feminine experience that many people do not see; they have been on the inside of it, and they have almost gone down with it. This wreck represents a whole different version of history than the one taught in school.

The history these girls have seen is not a sanctioned or redemptive history. It is, rather, a dangerous and unsettling history that happened beneath the boardwalk, beneath the house, beneath the trinities encouraged by the administrators in the counseling center, outside the pale of the women's magazines, outside the machine of what it was to be marriage material, outside the machine of feminism, outside the machine altogether. It is a basement history that eclipses the hopeful her-stories and histories we have been taught to believe and encouraged to memorize. It has occurred anyway, it is occurring now—if one listens closely, one can almost hear it below the surface.

Epilogue

This story began with the memory of a girl I never spoke to, even though I was curious about her and spent a long time dwelling in half-baked fantasies of her. Years after being in her presence, Anna still bothered me and appeared in my dreams like some version of female experience that I needed to understand. But there was no way of getting back to it: my curiosity was more of an irrational glimmer at the corner of my mind's eye.

When I first decided to reconsider and attempt to interpret the slut story, my idea was to write a profile of one girl. I planned to put out a query and then choose an individual who had the most compelling story. The story would be a vivid recounting of this girl's particular life in her particular school. But as my query was answered by more and more girls, it became impossible to narrow the story down; the story kept stretching further and further, without a horizon.

The girls echoed one another, resisted the realm of particularity, resisted any sort of reduction.

As I watched the story continually expand and extend its reach, as the phone continued to ring insistently, I had the vague and perhaps self-aggrandizing feeling that I was onto something as a journalist. I marched around with new purpose, harried, playing the role in my head of the newswoman about to crack the big story, the hard-nosed reporter with a flask in her desk chasing a big scoop.

The more obsessed I became with my big story, the more I talked about it to anyone who would listen. My sense of having a scoop was not shared by many of the people in my immediate surroundings, who were on the receiving end of my descriptions, diatribes, arguments for the story's vitality. "Oh, honey," my grandmother said, "I don't even know what you're saying!" Talking about it one day with a couple of male colleagues, I could not utter the word "slut" without both of them cracking up. It was like we were kids talking dirty. "Well, if you're gonna write about this," one said, finally able to repress his giggles, "you definitely need to talk about how much she liked it." "Yes, definitely," the other agreed. "These girls really bring it on themselves! And that needs to be addressed!"

These guys laughed into their coffee cups at the idea of the high school slut as a serious topic, and they looked at me like I was a little bit cracked. Although they could both immediately remember the first and last name of the slut of their schools, they did not think she merited this sort of consideration. Meanwhile, at home, the phone would ring with an occasional stray porn customer on the other end, a guy who said things like, "Hey, I saw your ad about sluts, and I thought maybe you're a slut? Maybe you like talking dirty?" I would hang up or not return their messages. Usually they wouldn't call again.

I tried to imagine where these misguided men would get the idea that a girl would take out a free phone line in her house just to talk dirty to them, and that she would do something as elaborate as present it as an author query. I tried to imagine the world they lived in, where this was a plausible expectation. Sometimes the heavy-breather calls would make me feel unaccountably lonely. They seemed to speak of a remarkable and untenable disconnection between desire and reality.

Strippers and sex trade workers often talk about the loneliness of their work; they describe the atmosphere of the topless club not as one of eroticism but as one of sadness. Male customers of prostitutes and strip bars have also described the loneliness of sitting there watching; they are given their ten minutes, and when the ten minutes are over, they are once again alone. The loneliness I felt when the heavy breathers called me was perhaps akin to the loneliness of the sex trade; you can hear the need in the voice, the sexual need in the room, but there is really nowhere for it to go, no way to really be released from it. People get so desperate that they will do anything to reenact the spectacle or the sound of connection.

I know you are a slut, so call me and talk to me about it.

Do you want to hear what I *did to the slut, the little whore, the little bitch?*

I know you like it.

These were the creepy, threatening reactions the call for high school sluts brought to the surface. It was no wonder that the girls I interviewed wanted to remain anonymous.

Nevertheless, despite the adverse reactions and the heavy

breathers, I couldn't help thinking of the high school slut as a story to end all stories. In my most delirious moments of excitement, I imagined the girls were prophetesses, like Cassandra, who no one would listen to or believe. But now I was listening. Maybe I was hungry for a spiritual connection and the girls who called me filled this hunger. They testified with such passion that to listen to them was to be converted to their vision of the world. I thought they were telling me something about the future, or they were letting me enter a realm that had previously been remote to me, ever since the days when Anna had seemed so remote and exotic in the hallway.

Teenagers live in a fugue state, halfway between consciousness and unconsciousness. They carry meanings up from the underworld of the collective mind and broadcast our fears back to us. To understand or at least address the virulence and violence of the slut story, teenagers and their graphic minds must be addressed without us laughing into our coffee cups. While the rumors kids pass on about what a slut is capable of might seem like ways of talking dirty that one eventually outgrows, really they're archetypal tales that illuminate the depths of the collective sexual imagination.

The pop culture icons embraced by girls in 2002 seem to indicate that notions of overly sexual "bad girls" are a thing of the past. Britney Spears and Christina Aguilera are the closest thing to strippers ever to be sold as teen songbirds. Indeed, in the hallways of high school now, girls more than ever dress as if they are asking for it, wearing half shirts that say FOXY or SEXY, piercing their navels, and tottering on high, chunky heels. (The flat-chested, prepubescent girls look particularly ridiculous in these getups.) But if styles have changed, and if Madeline's fishnets and cutoff T-shirts in the eighties wouldn't cause much of a stir now, the division between the girls still occurs. Thirteen- and fourteen-year-olds told me the same stories of being singled out by the football team rumors as forty-five- and fifty-year-olds did.

Jackie Gendel, twenty-six, came to me with living proof that the high school slut archetype is alive and well in modern America. In the on-line girl's magazine GURL.com, Jackie published a comic strip called *How My Friend Brenda Became the High School Slut.* Panel one reads: "When my best friend Brenda Jackson was in 7th grade, she looked like she was twenty. She was actually only 13. Sometimes she sounded like she was 40." Next a night is recounted when a group of boys "stood in line to get kisses from Brenda," after which all the girls reject Brenda. In the comic's last panel, the girls are calling Brenda "whore," while Brenda thinks "bores" to herself and walks away.

At the end of the strip, Jackie's e-mail address at GURL.com was printed, and just as I had been when I placed my query in the newspaper, Jackie was overwhelmed by the response. Her GURL folder nearly crashed under the weight of eight-hundred-plus e-mails.

Your friend Brenda needs to get her priorities straight! Girls who act like that only get what's coming to them.

Are you sure all she did was KISS them?

Why would you write a comic about something so stupid? Why are you wasting your talents?

I don't think your friend deserved to be called a slut. The same thing is happening to me in my school and I am really sick of it.

Many of the messages Jackie received asked for answers, but Jackie was so overwhelmed by the sheer number that she stopped trying to get back to everyone. Jackie had never published a comic on the Web before, and her e-mail had always been social or work related. Never before had she been on the receiving end of hundreds of random strangers' reactions. She had no idea what she was getting herself into with Brenda Jackson.

Yet no matter where and when she appears, the high school slut will create a reaction. Brenda, unleashed once again by Jackie's imagination, becomes the focus of the crowd's need. Now the Brenda gossip drifts in the ether of cyberspace, burning through its virtual hallways. Just like kids in school, the people who write to Jackie claim they could not *believe* her friend would do such things. They scold Brenda and are disgusted by her—they even try to give her bits of advice. ("Tell your friend to watch out or she will be a whore for good.") But Brenda wasn't even real; she was only a girl in a cartoon, permanently floating in GURL.com's vast memory.

I too sent e-mail to Jackie, and asked her to *write back please.* When she did, she gave me access to her unwieldy file of Brenda e-mails. A few months later, we met in a bar in New York. Although we had neglected to tell each other what we looked like, we immediately recognized each other. We were wearing the same kind of clothes ("Cool tights!" "I like your coat!"), and we both have a similar, slightly jumpy demeanor. It seems we are part of the same tribe.

While both Jackie and I have been actively remembering the high school slut, neither one of us knows where she is. As far as Jackie is concerned, Brenda is a memory more than a real person; her comic strip is drawn as if from the interior of memory. Now in her twenties, Jackie has started to wonder about the way she and her girlfriends blended together in their unanimous ostracism of Brenda. In the cartoon, the girls are drawn as if in a cocoon, all their bodies blending into the same flowered pattern, their heads distinct but their arms and legs attached. Exiled from them, Brenda is depicted alone in her body.

These are the pictures Jackie draws, trying to resurrect the past, give it form. The flood of e-mail made Jackie realize that Brenda was a dream in the mind of the world, too, and she asks, "Why would people get so worked up about my little comic?"

The way Jackie drew her, Brenda was full-lipped, wry, particular, but now she has become an archetype, a vessel through which people reassert their fear and loathing and desire.

In the bar, Jackie and I talked for a long time, eventually veering away from the topic of the high school slut. We started talking about people we know, and sure enough, because we are part of the same echelon of white America, we have a friend in common. We also find out we are both worshipers of Kathleen Hanna. Jackie tells me about Hanna's newest band, Le Tigre, and says that I must listen to it, that it absolutely rules.

When I emerged from drinks with Jackie, I felt like I had just had a great date. Although Jackie and I are the same type of girl, it is doubtful I would've met Jackie in a pre-Internet world. The spaces where we can explore what happened to us, where we can explore the depths and limits of our own tribes, are shifting rapidly with the advent of the Internet. Indeed, I think the idea of archetypes themselves, of a collective unconscious, has been transformed by this technological revolution. It is a whole new realm where one may bear witness to the wreck. The Internet is instant and anonymous, two qualities that make it a prime place for the oldest dreams in the world to flow unchecked, reaching their fullest and most arbitrary expression. It is also a place where connections with no tether to geography are made. When I connected with Jackie Gendel and she sent me her huge Brenda file, I found out more about the patterns of the high school slut myth than I ever would've on my own.

Just as they are in the hallway, what people are dying for in the space of the Net is a reaction. In the hallways, when the kids would yell "Whore" or "You want it," the ultimate goal was for the girl to swirl around and respond, for there to be a sign of life. This is also what people look for when they send e-mails out into space: that something will come back, someone will react, the girl will turn around and show herself.

If the myth is as strong as I've witnessed, is there any way to get out from beneath its shadows? Although it seems like myths will never lose their power, certain cultural signs show that tried-and-true facts can be exposed as rumors, archetypes can be released and taken apart. Maybe it is possible to get beyond them and see them for what they are: hallucinations formed by the head trip of patriarchy. Illusions.

In her groundbreaking book *Backlash*, Susan Faludi analyzed and deconstructed the phenomenon of the "man shortage." A popular topic in women's magazines marketed to the overthirty demographic, this shortage was supported by bogus statistics and frightening true-life stories of eternal singlehood. In article after article, women wrote about how it became impossible to find a man once you hit thirty because all the men after that point were "taken." There were simply not enough to go around. Faludi made mincemeat of the actual numbers. Her analysis revealed the man shortage to be a distracting scare tactic that pulled women away from their real work and their real power. Faludi saw the hysteria as part of a culture-wide backlash against the gains of the women's movement of the seventies. What Faludi evoked in a broad sense was the idea that when you live in a culture that places the man at the center, you begin to believe he can be stolen. The center does not hold, and so it is guarded in a panicked way. If you have been accused of stealing the man at the center, you feel like a fugitive. If you are trying to hold on to him, to prevent him from being stolen, you come up with all sorts of paranoid scenarios about the women in the darkness, the women in his darkest dreams. The man shortage is a fierce territoriality in which women scratch around for space, trying to fight off other women so their own man will not be taken away.

The fear that there are not enough men is certainly related to the fear that there's a girl out there who wants "too much" sex. These are vaguely quantitative ways of thinking based in a boy-crazy, voodoo economy wherein monogamous heterosexual love carries an ultimate value. When Faludi exposed the man shortage myth she hollowed out one of the basic tenets of this economy. She took apart an old standard by which women had judged one another, a belief that had prevented women from looking directly at one another and had kept them in a state of war readiness.

Myths are taken apart and the horizon shifts. Maybe there is a trickle-down effect; maybe the boy-crazy wars of the hallway will become more and more halfhearted as the mechanisms that drive them are exposed. Girls emerge who signify a shift, like Kathleen Hanna, marching around with the word SLUT on her stomach, as if to say, *You cannot name me anymore, I have already named myself.*

One more sign of the changing times is a potboiler movie with a feminist twist called *The Contender.* Released in 2000 to mildly successful box office numbers, *The Contender* told the story of a Democratic female vice presidential nominee who is almost brought down by her Republican foes over a sex scandal. Nominee Lane Hanson, played by actress Joan Allen, confronts rumors that she participated in a "gang bang" in college; there are even pictures shown in short flashes across the screen with the woman's face never revealed. These pictures find their way to the hands of Hanson's nemesis and the head of the Senate committee approving her appointment. Gary Oldman plays the doddering Republican who is outraged and delighted over the gang bang photographs. He brandishes them while railing about family values, islands of spit forming at the corners of his mouth. He interviews "witnesses" who say they heard from a friend that Lane Hanson was "covered with cum" after the event.

What's remarkable about *The Contender* is how our heroine chooses to handle these accusations: she refuses to dignify them with an answer. When asked repeatedly if the gang bang "really happened," Hanson declares, "I will not dignify this. I won't go there." Maybe this seems so remarkable because of the way Joan Allen plays it: dressed in expensive suits, standing with perfect posture, with a mischievous gleam in her eye that says, *What if I did?* Throughout the film, she never answers the question of her involvement. Her enemies predictably become more and more apoplectic.

The sex scandal in *The Contender* is one more version of the train job legend, but here the rumor spreads in the White House, evoking the Clinton sex scandals of the late nineties. The film's themes of corruption and sexual hypocrisy in the secret world of Washington specifically evoked Monicagate. But *The Contender* also raises broader questions that relate back to the stories of the girls I interviewed: Why does the train job rumor have the power to bring down a life? Why are women sent through this ring of fire, this great indignity? Caught in the grip of the rumor, our heroine keeps her cool. And she never tells anyone what she has done or where she has been.

In *The Contender*, the woman with the train job rumor in her past has succeeded and now she wears a flawless suit. She ends up being vindicated by the committee, and it's implied that the girl in the train job photos was not her. But the viewer's never sure what she was doing, and the film becomes a comment on our vast curiosity about what she might have been doing. Her eyes have a self-possessed and contained intelligence. She seems like she could easily be a president.

The movie seems to carry some hope for the future. It makes me contemplate the possibility of getting out of the story as it has been told, as it has been rumored. One night I have a dream that seems to speak of an ideal time to come.

This dream occurs a few days after I talked to Kate, the woman who was raped beneath the boardwalk in Jersey. As I remember it, I am under a boardwalk, too, although it is not as dark as the place Kate described—light comes in from gaps in the floorboards. I can see the ocean through the gaps. I am down there with my tape recorder, and girls hover all around me, although they are at a distance. The closer I look, the more I realize the shadows are overrun with them. All the girls wear the same leather jacket with the word WHORES sewn on the back.

Above the boardwalk, people can be detected flying kites or rolling babies in carriages. The surf comes in, but the daylight people don't pay any attention to it. Meanwhile, underneath the boardwalk, I try to get the girls to talk to me. I hold out my machine and say, "Wait, wait," but they don't pay any attention. They are too busy, too preoccupied with whatever it is they're doing or planning. They speak to one another in hand signals, code words, monotones. They are a gang, a mob—the Whores. The girls in my interviews have become their own crowd, instead of the ones singled out by the crowd.

I am not allowed any interviews in this dream world. The time to talk about what it was like has passed. Now there is too much work to be done, too many gang activities to organize. When I look back at the dream I realize what is missing under the boardwalk is the sense of loneliness. Loneliness has been replaced by this resourceful humming, the buzz of plans being made.

This story began with a girl I did not know. Now it ends in a multitude of voices, in a place where people keep dreaming themselves out of the old world, out of the past, out of the seemingly insurmountable slut era. Girls in the midst of it now are constructing shields that are starting to work—the shield of the tough ball-buster act and the jacket worn like armor, and the shield of language itself: *No, I will not consider that. I will not dignify that story.* Maybe as the slut story comes further into consciousness, what will happen when it is spoken, when the rumors are formulated, will be a gradual release in the tension of the archetype, like a balloon losing its helium and coming slowly down to earth. As the archetype succumbs to gravity, the rumors will not flow so freely or so quickly; when one is in the midst of them, one will be aware that a cliché is being reenacted. Maybe ideals of dignity and notions of shame will be transformed. I won't presume to imagine what will happen. In the meantime, the girls keep calling. They keep sending messages.

Bibliography

Beauvoir, Simone de. *The Second Sex.* Knopf, 1968.

Boyer, Paul, and Stephen Nissenbaum. *Salem Possessed: The Social Origins of Witchcraft.* Harvard University Press, 1974.

Brown, Lyn Mikel, and Carol Gilligan. *Meeting at the Crossroads: Women's Psychology and Girls' Development.* Harvard University Press, 1992.

Brumberg, Joan Jacobs. *The Body Project: An Intimate History of American Girls.* Vintage, 1998.

Canetti, Elias. *Crowds and Power.* Noonday Press, 1960.

Coles, Robert, and Geoffrey Stokes. *Sex and the American Teenager.* Rolling Stone Press, 1985.

Davis, Angela Y. *Women, Race, and Class.* Random House, 1981.

Dijkstra, Bram. *Evil Sisters: The Threat of Female Sexuality and the Cult of Manhood.* Knopf, 1996.

Dinsmore, Christine. *From Surviving to Thriving: Incest, Feminism and Recovery.* State University of New York Press, 1991.

Dworkin, Andrea. *Intercourse.* Free Press, 1987.

Echols, Alice. *Scars of Sweet Paradise: The Life and Times of Janis Joplin.* Metropolitan Books, Henry Holt and Co., 1999.

Eisler, Riane. *The Chalice and the Blade.* HarperCollins, 1987.

Faludi, Susan. *Backlash: The Undeclared War Against American Women.* Crown Publishers, 1991.

Foucault, Michel. *The History of Sexuality.* Vol. 1. Vintage, 1990.

Freud, Sigmund. *The Basic Writings of Sigmund Freud.* Translated by A. A. Brill. Modern Library, 1938.

Friedan, Betty. *The Feminine Mystique.* Reprint edition. Laurel/Dell, 1984.

Gaines, Donna. *Teenage Wasteland: Suburbia's Dead End Kids.* HarperCollins, 1990.

Gates, Henry Louis, Jr., and Cornel West. *The Future of the Race.* Knopf, 1996.

Haraway, Donna J. *Simians, Cyborgs, and Women: The Reinvention of Nature.* Routledge, 1991.

Hildebrand, Dietrich von. *In Defense of Purity: An Analysis of the Catholic Ideals of Purity and Virginity.* Franciscan Herald Press, 1930.

hooks, bell. *Ain't I a Woman: Black Women and Feminism.* South End Press, 1981.

———. *Bone Black: Memories of Childhood.* Henry Holt, 1996.

———. *Sisters of the Yam: Black Women and Self-Recovery.* South End Press, 1993.

Irigaray, Luce. *This Sex Which Is Not One.* Translated by Catherine Porter. Cornell University Press, 1985.

Jung, C. G. *The Archetypes and the Collective Unconscious.* Translated by R. F. C. Hull. Princeton University Press, 1959.

———. *Aspects of the Feminine.* Translated by R. F. C. Hull. Princeton University Press, 1982.

Kempe, Ruth S., and C. Henry. *The Common Secret: Sexual Abuse of Children and Adolescents.* W. H. Freeman and Co., 1984.

Kinsey, Alfred C. *Sexual Behavior in the Human Female.* Saunders, 1953.

Kozol, Jonathan. *Amazing Grace.* Crown, 1995.

———. *Death at an Early Age.* Reprint edition. New American Library, 1990.

Lay, Wilfred. *Man's Unconscious Passion.* Dodd Mead, 1920.

Lefkowitz, Bernard. *Our Guys: The Glen Ridge Rape and the Secret Life of the Perfect Suburb.* Vintage, 1997.

Luker, Kristen. *Dubious Conceptions: The Politics of Teenage Pregnancy.* Harvard University Press, 1996.

Malcolm, Janet. *The Journalist and the Murderer.* Vintage, 1990.

Males, Mike. *The Scapegoat Generation: America's War on Adolescents.* Common Courage Press, 1996.

The Malleus Maleficarum of Heinrich Kramer and James Sprenger. Translated with an introduction by the Reverend Montague Summers. Dover Publications, 1971.

Marcuse, Herbert. *Eros and Civilization: A Philosophical Inquiry into Freud.* Beacon Press, 1955.

Marks, Elaine, and Isabelle de Courtivron, eds. *New French Feminisms: An Anthology.* University of Massachussetts Press, 1980.

Millett, Kate. *Sexual Politics.* Touchstone, 1990.

Moi, Toril. *French Feminist Thought.* Blackwell, 1987.

———. *Sexual/Textual Politics.* Methuen, 1985.

Nathanson, Constance A. *Dangerous Passage: The Social Control of Sexuality in Women's Adolescence.* Temple University Press, 1991.

Rich, Adrienne. *On Lies, Secrets, and Silence: Selected Prose 1966–1978.* Norton, 1979.

———. *Poems Selected and New, 1950–1974.* Norton, 1975.

Rowbotham, Sheila. *A History of Women.* Penguin, 1997.

The Salem Witchcraft Papers. Vol. 2, 1692. Da Capo Press, 1977.

Shibutani, Tamotsu. *Improvised News: A Sociological Study of Rumor.* Bobbs-Merrill Company, 1966.

Showalter, Elaine. *Hystories: Hysterical Epidemics and Modern Media.* Columbia University Press, 1997.

Snitow, Ann, Christine Stansell, and Sharon Thompson, eds. *Powers of Desire: The Politics of Sexuality.* Monthly Review Press, 1983.

The Sorenson Report: Adolescent Sexuality in Contemporary America. World Publishing, 1973.

Tanenbaum, Leora. *Slut! Growing Up Female with a Bad Reputation.* Seven Stories Press, 1999.

Thompson, Sharon. *Going All the Way: Teenage Girls' Tales of Sex, Romance, and Pregnancy.* Hill and Wang, 1996.

Wolf, Naomi. *Promiscuities: The Secret Struggle for Womanhood.* Random House, 1997.

Young-Bruehl, Elisabeth, ed. *Freud on Women: A Reader.* Norton, 1990.

SOURCES

For invaluable documents from feminism's Second Wave I used the Duke University on-line archival collection "Documents from the Women's Liberation Movement," http://scriptorium.lib.duke.edu/wlm/.

David Grad was quoted from an unpublished introduction to Joel Schalit, *Jerusalem Calling* (Akashic Press, 2001).

Acknowledgments

Thanks first and foremost to the girls and women who agreed to talk to me for this project. I'm awed by their generosity and eloquence. My hilarious former office mate at *The Stranger,* Dan Savage, first placed the query and pushed me to pursue this project. My agent, Bill Clegg, gave passionate support and remarkable insight. My editor, Gillian Blake, was both tough and nurturing—I'm lucky to have her voice in my head. Rachel Sussman at Scribner asked crucial questions at the crux of revision. Tim Keck gave me a great job and a place where I could get fired up. My family gave me early momentum.

Thanks to Jackie Gendel for Brenda and all she evoked.

Thanks to Budget Suites of America right behind the Stardust, Las Vegas, Nevada. Thanks to the Wallace Stegner Fellowships, the Hedgebrook Colony, the Richard Hugo House, and the Washington Artist Trust.

For encouragement and inspiration thanks to Julia White, Ivy Meeropol, Rosemary Harer, Gil Sorrentino, Ann Powers, Wendy Salinger, Paul Tough, Steve Erickson, R. J. Smith, Kit Rachlis, Trisha Ready, Matthew Stadler, Stacey Levine, A. J. Jimenez, Angela Medina, Roberta Brown Root, Riz Rollins, and Jenny Offill.

And thanks most of all to Rich Jensen, for everything.

QUESTIONS FOR DISCUSSION

1. (Throughout *Fast Girls*, Emily White offers explanations for why high school students label a particular girl a "slut." She posits that in part, these rumors can spring out of teenagers' fear and ignorance of sex: "Kids tell slut stories because they need an allegory for the mystery of sex itself" (12). The compulsion to discuss taboo subjects and general teen boredom and malaise are other factors White sites. Do you agree with these origin theories? What other reasons might there be?

2. After talking to numerous women who had been named their high school's slut, White noticed a pattern of traits these women shared: they were generally extroverted, suburban white girls who had experienced precocious puberty and often had a history of sexual abuse. What do you make of these traits, especially the disturbing history of sexual abuse? If you knew of a high school "slut," did she fit the "type"? Did you know someone who met this profile—or even was in fact promiscuous—yet escaped being branded a slut? Why do you think that was?

3. White explores the idea that the slut is an archetype in the Jungian sense and therefore embedded in the collective conscience (or at least, the conscience of a specific American socioeconomic group, e.g., white suburban America). Do you agree with this idea?

4. The author found through her research that women from backgrounds other than white suburbia often used different terminology to describe the "slut" of their school. Some of the nonwhite "sluts" the author spoke with had a different—and less negative—experience of being the "slut" than the white girls; they did not feel isolated nor were they treated cruelly by classmates. How do you explain these findings? What do you think about White's comment that racial and sexual insults are sometimes paired in high schools as "parallel hateful languages" (169)? White notes that "far more white women responded to [her] survey than nonwhite women" (163). Why does the word "slut" resonate with white suburban girls almost exclusively? Is suburban, predominantly white America a unique social system that engenders the phenomenon of the slut? Why or why not?

5. White touches upon the difference between the sexual education of boys and that of girls as created and perpetuated by American media culture. White notes that while boys have access to pornography and an interest in it is seen as a "rite of passage" (57), girls are given only "hints, romance tips, and teen idols. A graphic discussion of sex has no real place in adolescent feminine development" (58). Do you agree with the author's assertions? How do you see media and culture affecting gender roles and informing what is considered appropriate sexual behavior—for boys, for girls, for men, for women? How do you think the dissimilarities in how boys and girls are taught about sex relate to the creation of the slut myth in high school? Note that White found that both boys and girls could generate the slut rumor about a girl in their school; what part do you think each gender's knowledge about sex plays in creating these rumors?

6. How does the presence of the slut (and the slut as a "category" of one person) fit into or disrupt the carefully-constructed high

school social system? How is the slut both powerful and weak? How do some of the sluts profiled in the book seek to create power for themselves, in both destructive and positive ways?

7. Certainly many of the women profiled in *Fast Girls* were treated with varying degrees of brutality by their classmates. From where do you think this need for violently lashing out at the "slut" stems? What do the teenagers perpetrating the violence hope to accomplish? Why does the author, and why do you, think that girls are more malicious than boys toward the slut? In the end, do you agree with the author that "high school is such a clear spectacle of cruelty" (32)?

8. Do you feel that the creation of the slut myth is strictly a teenage/high school phenomenon? Why or why not? How would you explain the process of how and why certain women receive a "bad" reputation in college or even in adult life? Are such women instead classified as "players" or "promiscuous" because of their age, and how do such names differ from the label of "slut"? How are such adult women treated differently than the high school girls by other women? By men?

9. White talks about how on the *Dr. Laura* show, "women are either mothers or sluts" (99). Discuss women's struggle with the middle ground between being—or being perceived as—a "bad girl" or a "good girl." White notes that in a March 1999 *Cosmopolitan* magazine reader survey, many respondents advised women to lie about their number of sexual partners, skewing lower than the truth (119). How do you feel about this suggestion? Do you agree with the observation made by many of the girls White interviewed that ' "the girls are sluts, the boys are studs' " (90)? Why is there no male counterpart to the "loose woman"?

10. How do you view the women profiled in *Fast Girls*—as deserving of what they got? As victims? As weak? As powerful? What do you think of them in terms of their diversity, their feelings about being named the slut, their agendas, their experiences in adulthood? How did the label change them, in both positive and negative ways? Why did some of the sluts begin to feel "like a man" (101)? Were these girls indeed "born into the wrong gender" (102)? Why or why not? What do you make of the fact that some of the women felt "devalued" for the rest of their lives and were unable to have normal romantic relationships?

11. White discusses throughout *Fast Girls* how many of the "sluts" became disassociated from their "real" selves because they were being defined and objectified by others (109). White wonders whether her interviews of these women were in fact a new process of objectification: "Was I engaged in one more form of writing what I wanted to about her, only this time not on the bathroom wall?" (111). How would you answer the author's question?

12. White admits that she did *not* "check out these women's pasts" because she was "far more interested in the narratives surrounding her than in figuring out whether or not she deserved her reputation" (60). If the interviews had theoretically been expanded to encompass the women's families/friends/classmates, what do you think those people would have said? Would these auxiliary voices expand your understanding of why the myth of the slut was generated in each case, or do you agree with the author that it is more crucial to focus on how the "slut" herself perceived, felt about, and handled the label? Do you think White was indeed told the truth by these women?

13. The author discusses the assumptions and biases she brought to the research; she states she "projected [her] own disposition onto